Holland Lop Rabbit.

Holland Lop Rabbits as pets.

Holland Lop Rabbit book for pros and cons, care, housing, cost, diet and health.

By

Macy Peterson

ALL RIGHTS RESERVED. This book contains material protected under International and Federal Copyright Laws and Treaties.

Any unauthorized reprint or use of this material is strictly prohibited. No part of this book may be reproduced or transmitted in any form or by any means, electronic, mechanical or otherwise, including photocopying or recording, or by any information storage and retrieval system without express written permission from the author.

Copyright © 2018

Published by: Pesa Publishing

Table of Contents

Table of Contents 3

Introduction 4

Chapter 1: Understanding a Holland Lop rabbit 6

Chapter 2: Things to know before you buy a Holland Lop rabbit 18

Chapter 3: Handling a Holland Lop rabbit 33

Chapter 4: Habitat requirements 41

Chapter 5: Meeting the nutritional requirements of the Holland Lop rabbit 62

Chapter 6: Maintaining health of the Holland Lop rabbit 71

Chapter 7: Training the Holland Lop rabbit 96

Chapter 8: Grooming and showing the Holland Lop rabbit 102

Conclusion 112

References 113

Introduction

I want to thank you and congratulate you for buying this book. This book will help you to understand everything you need to know about domesticating a Holland Lop rabbit. You will learn all the aspects related to raising the Holland Lop rabbit successfully at home. You will be able to understand the pros and cons, behavior, basic care, keeping, housing, diet and health related to the animal.

There are people who are impressed by the adorable looks of the Holland Lop rabbit. They think that this reason is enough to domesticate the animal, but the domestication of a Holland Lop rabbit has its unique challenges and issues. If you are not ready for these challenges, then you are not ready to domesticate the animal. If you have already bought or adopted Holland Lop rabbit, even then you need to understand your pet so that you take care of him or her in a better way. It is important that you understand that owning any pet will have its advantages and disadvantages.

You should see whether with all its pros and cons, the animal fits well into your household. Domesticating and taming a pet is not only fun, there is a lot of hard work that goes into it. It is important that you are ready to commit before you decide to domesticate the animal. If you are a prospective buyer, understanding these points will help you to make a wise decision. When you decide to hand raise a Holland Lop rabbit, you will be flooded with questions. Would I be able to care for him? Would I be able to domesticate a wild animal? What if I fail in my endeavor? You will find yourself thinking about these and many such questions.

Not matter how scared you are, you can always make it work if you equip yourself with the right knowledge. If you understand how a Holland Lop rabbit should be cared for, you will make it work for yourself. You should make all possible efforts to understand the basic requirements of your pet. There are a few basic requirements that you will have to fulfill. Even if you can't afford to give the pet too much luxury, you should be able to take care of his basic requirements.

If you wish to raise a Holland Lop rabbit as a pet, there are many things that you need to keep in mind. It can get very daunting for a new owner. Because of the lack of information, you will find yourself getting confused as to what should be done and what should be avoided. You might be confused and scared, but there is no need to feel so confused.

Once you form a relationship with the Holland Lop rabbit, it gets better and easier for you as the owner. The pet will grow up to be friendly and adorable. He/she will also value the bond as much as you do. This will be good for the pet and also for you as the pet owner in the long run.

Chapter 1: Understanding a Holland Lop rabbit

One of the characteristic features of the Holland Lop rabbits is that they have pendulous ears. It should be noted that this species of rabbit is said to resemble the dwarfed lop rabbit. These rabbits are also small in size. They are very compact and tiny. The adult mature body weighs up to five pounds.

The Holland Lop rabbit is a small rabbit which has lopped ears, hence the name 'Holland Lop'. It should also be noted here that in the United Kingdom, there is a very popular breed of domestic rabbits that are called miniature lops. It is similar to the Holland Lop.

It is known that these rabbits are very gentle and friendly in their demeanour. They are attractive and playful in nature. These rabbits are available in many colours. This is an advantage for people looking for a colour of their choice.

There are many breeds of rabbits all over the world. The ARBA, which is the American Rabbit Breeders' Association, has already recognised over forty eight breeds of rabbits. On the other hand, the BRC, which is the British Rabbit Council, recognises over sixty breeds of rabbits.

It should be noted here that there could be several more breeds of rabbits that are still not recognised by the ARBA or BRC. There are many lop rabbit breeds amongst the rabbits. The Holland Lop is one these breeds.

Of all the breeds that are recognised all over the world, there are over nineteen breeds of lop rabbits. The term lop is used to describe a special type of ear in the rabbits. There are many breeds that are grouped together under the lop rabbit breeds.

It should be noted here that the deciding common factor amongst the lop rabbits is the shape of the ear. The various breeds grouped under the lop rabbits can differ in various parameters, such as colour and fur.

1. What are lop rabbits?

It should be noted that lop rabbits is not a specific breed of rabbits. It is only a certain kind and type of rabbits. There're further many breeds under this category. Any rabbit, irrespective of its breed, which has ears hanging from the head is called a lop rabbit.

Most rabbit breeds have ears that stand up straight. The ears are mostly small in size and look like little bells hanging from the head of the animal.

Lop rabbits can also be called lop eared rabbits. Lop rabbits are known to be friendly and cuddly by nature. But they require a lot of attention from your side. Any person who is not ready for the huge responsibility should not get a lop rabbit. They will require a lot of time and care from your side.

If you have the time and the energy to look after the lop rabbits, they can prove to be great pets. It has been stated earlier that there are over nineteen breeds of lop rabbits. It should be noted here that not all of them are recognised by the ARBA and the BRC.

In the United States, the ARBA recognised five breeds of lop rabbits. On the other hand, the BRC recognises nine breeds of lop eared rabbits.

The five breeds of lop rabbits recognised by the ARBA are American fuzzy lop, English lop, French lop, Holland Lop and Miniature lop. The nine breeds of lop eared rabbits recognised by the BRC are the Cashmere lop, Cashmere miniature lop, Dwarf lop, English lop, French lop, German lop, Meissner lop, Miniature lop and Miniature lion lop.

There are different ways to differentiate between various lop eared rabbits. One of the most common ways to do so is to take the fur type into consideration. There are many rabbits that have velvety and short fur.

There are some rabbits which have long fur. A rabbit can also have medium type of fur. You can also use the shape of the rabbit as a parameter to distinguish between the various breeds of the same type.

Rabbits can also be categorised by the purpose they solve. Based on this criteria, there are three main types of rabbits; fur, meat and fur. The breeds that serve different purposes differ from each other in the way they look.

It is known that the breeds of rabbit meant for meat grow very quickly. They are large in their appearance. Such rabbits attain maturity by the age of eight to twelve weeks. They are ready to be used as meat by this time.

There are certain breeds of rabbits that are bred because of the quality of their fur. This fur is further used for clothes and coats. There are certain fur rabbits that are also meat rabbits. There are other types that are very popular for their fur.

2. What is a Holland Lop rabbit?

The Holland Lop rabbit is not yet recognised by the British Rabbit Council which is also popularly known as the BRC. But, it is recognised by the American Rabbit Breeders Association (ARBA).

It should be noted here that the miniature lop rabbit is known to be quite similar to the Holland Lop rabbit, though the former is smaller in size. The miniature lop is recognised by the BRC.

The country of origin of the Holland Lop is the Netherlands. These rabbits are also called the dwarf lops or the Netherland dwarf lops.

The Holland Lop rabbit is a very popular breed of domestic rabbits which is found in United States of America. If you see the smallest of rabbits in the lop eared rabbits category, Holland Lop rabbit is the smallest of them all.

The rabbit stays small its entire life. This makes it ideal for people that do not have much space in their house but still wish to pet a rabbit. It can make an ideal pet if you can give your time and attention to the Holland Lops rabbit.

If you are a prospective owner of the Holland Lop rabbit then this section will help you to learn more about the Holland Lop rabbit. You will learn some interesting facts about the rabbit.

The Holland Lop are classified under medium sized rabbits. They do not grow too big in size. This is in tune with the body structure of the animal.

3. History of the Holland Lop rabbit

It is known that the Holland Lop rabbit has a tie with the American fuzzy lop rabbit in terms of size.

Adrain De Cock is said to be the original breeder of the Holland Lop rabbits. He was looking to produce a smaller version of the French lop rabbit.

In 1949, during the winter months, he bred a Netherland dwarf doe and a French lop buck. The litter that he obtained was not of good quality.

Then he switched the sexes of the bunnies and tried again. He got a litter of six bunnies which had normal erect ears.

In the year 1952, he bred an English lop buck with one of the does in the litter that he produced. He got a litter of five this time with mixed characteristics of erect, lopped and half lopped bunnies.

Next a half lopped doe from this batch was bred with a buck from the previous batch of litters. The results were highly awaited. This led to further enhancements of characteristic features.

By this mechanism, he arrived at the Holland Lop rabbit species. The original batch weighed anywhere between 2.5 kilograms to 3 kilograms.

Further breeding was done in January 1964 to arrive at bunnies that weighed around 2kgs and not more than that.

The bunny was presented to the Netherlands governing rabbit council. It is then that the Holland Lop rabbit was recognised as a new breed of lop eared bunnies.

Aleck Brooks brought this new breed of bunnies to the United States in the year 1976. Three years later, in 1979, ARBA recognised this rabbit breed.

4. Body structure

Holland Lop rabbits are very small in size. They are in fact amongst the smallest of rabbits. The Holland Lop rabbit has a compact body and curved profile and its legs are short and rounded.

Size of the bunny

Holland Lop bunnies are dwarfs. A fully grown adult can weight 2-4 pounds.

Weight

If you are planning to show your junior Holland Lop rabbit then the rabbit should be well under the age of six months. The weight should be 2 pounds or more.

Similarly, a senior Holland Lop rabbit is six months or older in age. The weight of the senior bunny should be between 2-4 pounds.

Shape

The Holland Lop rabbit is well balanced in its length, breadth and depth. It is very compact to look at and is also heavy muscled.

Take a look at the Holland Lops rabbit, and you will realise that the bunny has a short, thick set and massive look.

The hind quarters of the bunny rabbit are deep, broad and very well filled at the low portions of the hind quarters.

The shoulders are very deep and are carried back to the hind quarters. The chest of the rabbit is well filled and is broad.

If the width is checked, it can be seen that the width of the shoulders is almost equal but never more than the width of the hind quarters.

Ears

As mentioned earlier, the ears are the most significant feature of a lop eared rabbit breed. They are also a make or break factor when you are showing your pet in different shows.

The ARBA has kept a total of 42 points out of the 100 for the ears, head and crown of the Holland Lop rabbit.

The shape of the crown and the head effect the ears because of their lop nature. The ears are rounded at the tips and are short.

The shape of the ear of the Holland Lop rabbit can be compared to a teaspoon. The ear is wide and open up against the head of the bunny.

If the ear falls very long, more than one inch of the chin, then it will be difficult to show these kinds of rabbits in shows.

Fur/coat of the Holland Lop rabbit

The fur of the Holland Lop rabbit is fine, dense and glossy. It is good in texture and very uniform in its length.

The fur is one inch in its length. It is roll backed from the hind quarters to the shoulders of the bunny.

The flesh is very firm. The coat is set in the pelt. The coat is of a very good quality and is neither too thick nor too thin.

5. Lifespan

On average, your Holland Lop rabbit can live up to 10 years. The lifespan can increase by 3-4 year if the pet is kept indoors and is kept well.

6. Purpose and breed status

The purpose behind producing Holland Lop rabbits was to create a show breed with a small size. This is the main factor.

These rabbits are undoubtedly very popular on show tables. But, they also make good companion rabbit and house pet.

These rabbits are not rare. In fact, it is known that their popularity is increasing by the day. It will be very easy for you to find a breeder of Holland Lop rabbits in your vicinity.

7. Personality

It might not be right to generalise the qualities of the Holland Lop rabbit because each bunny is unique in its own way.

But, it is important to understand the characteristics of an animal in regards to its entire species. This will help you to understand the pet better and will also help you to make an informed decision whether you want to keep the Holland Lop or not.

The Holland Lop rabbits are very smart and intelligent. They are easy to train. You would be delighted to know that slowly these animals are becoming very popular as pets.

The bunny is known to have a rather excellent temperament. They are not very aggressive and are known to be gentle and docile in nature.

They are a good breed to have when you have kids in the household. They are also easy to train and handle.

Bucks

The male rabbit is known as the buck. The buck Holland Lop rabbit is known to be cuddlier in comparison to the the female Holland Lop rabbit.

If you have to choose between a buck and a doe, then a buck will be a better pet. He is less likely to go in depression when compared with the female bunny.

The bucks love to gain attention. In nature, it is more like a pet dog. If you have a doe that is in heat, you can expect your pet buck to spray.

Does

The female rabbit is known as the doe. The doe Holland Lop rabbit is known to be less cuddly in comparison to the the male Holland Lop rabbit.

The doe can have more mood swings when compared with the male Holland Lop rabbit. Otherwise, they are very docile in their temperament.

The doe is most likely to be grumpy when it is in heat. Some of them might even grunt and box.

8. Holland Lop rabbit varieties

The Holland Lop rabbit breed is found in many varieties of colours. You should know that at present 84 colours are already recognised.

If you are looking at showing your Holland Lop rabbit then you should know that ARBA recognised only two groups; Broken and Solid.

Holland Lop rabbit colors

As stated earlier, the Holland Lop rabbits are available in many colors. This gives the rabbit lover a chance to choose from his favourite colors. This section will help you understand the colors and patterns that your Holland Lop rabbit can come in.

Self

The self-colored type refers to the rabbit that has a single color all over the body. This means that a single color will be seen on the body, limbs, head and ears of the animal. The various colors in this pattern are white, blue, chocolate and black.

Agouti

This pattern has typically three or even more colors. There is a dark base color and alternating colors run through the base color.

The top of the rabbit and the side of the rabbit are said to be ticked and banded. You will notice that the tip of the various hairs is of a different color. The various colors in this pattern include chestnut, opal and chinchilla.

Shaded

In this type, there is a main color. There is a gradual change from this main color, as the shade keeps getting lighter. The sides and belly typically have the lighter shade of color. The various colors in this pattern include sable medium, sable light, smoke pearl and chocolate point.

Broken

This is one of the most common categories in the Holland Lop rabbits. A Holland Lop rabbit is said to belong to the broken color category when the rabbit has a combination of two colors, white color and any other color.

The color of the body of the rabbit is broken in an even pattern. There is color around the eyes and ears of the rabbit and also around the nose. The Holland Lops exhibiting this pattern are also called broken lops.

The color possessed by the broken lops is anywhere between ten percent and seventy percent. Generally, there is a marking on the nose which is called the butterfly marking. This marking is outlined by the color white.

The circles around the ears and the eyes are of a different color. It is also seen that the front feet of the Holland Lop are white. The back feet may be colored or may also be white. These are some of the general characteristics of the broken category in the Holland Lop rabbits.

Ticked

This is another category of the Holland Lop rabbits. A Holland Lop rabbit belongs to this category if the tips of its hairs are of a different from the color of its body. It is said that the bunnies in the ticked category have the steel gene.

These rabbits can possess ticking in silver or in gold. If you wish to know the colors that this category holds, the you should know that you can get a Holland Lop bunny in smoke, sable, silver fox, lilac, chocolate, blue and also black.

Wide band

A Holland Lop rabbit with the wide band will look quite similar to the one in the agouti category. But, there are a couple of differences that separate the two patterns. While the secondary color shows around the ears, tail and eyes in the agouti, it shows in a layer in the wide band pattern.

A Holland Lop rabbit belonging to this particular category will have a particular color at the top. There will be another color at the bottom part of the bunny's body.

The colors that you can expect to find in the white band category are fawn, orange, red, frosty and cream.

9. Pros and cons of keeping Holland Lop rabbits

If you wish to hand raise an animal, you should make sure that you understand the characteristics and the requirements of the animal. When you domesticate the Holland Lop rabbit, you will face many pros and cons along the way.

This section will help you understand the pros and cons of keeping a Holland Lop rabbit at home.

Pros of keeping a Holland Lop rabbit at home

There are many pros of keeping a Holland Lop rabbit:

- These rabbits enjoy the company of human beings and are known to have a good time with them.

- These pets are great for smaller living spaces, such as a flat or small house.

- These pets are generally low maintenance. They do not need frequent baths, which can be a great relief for a caregiver.

- A rabbit is a very intelligent and smart animal. You can easily train him/her to suit your family and living conditions.

- The rabbit is beautiful to look at. If you are fond of beautiful looking pets, then this rabbit is definitely the pet for you and your family.

- The rabbits are very energetic and lively pets. They are very active during the early hours of the morning and evening.

- The rabbits are very sweet, entertaining and gentle in their nature, yet they need to be trained well so that they don't get too mischievous. You will also get to see the calm, composed and gentle side of the animal.

- If they are raised to be social, they will be very social. You should make sure that they spend a lot of time indoors with the family members. This will only help in being more social and affectionate.

- The rabbit is a very playful, happy-go-lucky kind of animal. The rabbit likes having fun and can be a constant source of entertainment for everyone in the family.

- You can enter your pet in various shows that happen everywhere. These are shows that can help you gain popularity and can help you win also.

- They are capable of forming strong emotional bonds. These bonds will last for a lifetime. You need to spend quality time with your pet to form such strong bonds.

- You will find it easier to groom the pet because he/she will be relaxed and calm, unlike many other pets that don't allow the owners to groom them.

- It has been established over the years that the rabbits are easy to train.

- When you domesticate a rabbit, you will have to worry less about diet. This is because nowadays many diet mixtures and pellets are available commercially. These food items ensure that the right nutrition is given to your beloved pet. You can be happy because you can save yourself from the tension of preparing food mixes for the pet every now and then.

- You would have to be extra careful and cautious while taking care of the bunny, but when all the precautions are taken, it is a very much possible task to hand raise a bunny.

- They will respond to the way you choose to communicate with them. If you provide good training to your rabbit, you will notice that he/she responds well. In due time and over the course of the training, the pet will also start obeying some simple commands that you would want them to obey.

Cons of keeping a Holland Lop rabbit at home

There are many cons of keeping a Holland Lop rabbit:

- The Holland Lop rabbit can get nervous and frightened very easily. They can get uneasy and can slip into depression if not looked after.

- These rabbits enjoy the company of human beings and are known to have a good time with them. But, they should be trained to socialize from an early age. If they don't socialize from the beginning, they can develop aggression towards human beings and other animals.

- Bigger animals can make the Holland Lop rabbit prey.

- You can't keep these animals in a cage at all times. They need space and time to explore and play.

- If the rabbit is not under supervision, it can get very mischievous. The animal will chew at things, even electrical wiring.

- The pet is also prone to many diseases. The caregiver will have to be very careful with the health of the pet.

- The pet can get stressed and depressed if it is left lonely for long durations. You can't leave it in the cage for too long.

- The bunnies love to dig in the ground. In fact, the rabbit will try to dig everywhere. If the pet is left on its own, it might try to dig in your sofas, beds, etc.

- If you don't have the time and energy to spend on grooming a pet, then the Holland Lop rabbit is not the right pet for you.

- If the children of the house are not careful, they can scare the pet. This can be detrimental to the Holland Lop rabbit.

- The cost that you will incur while buying and raising is more when compared to other pets, such as the dog and the cat. If spending too much money is an issue with you, then you will have to think twice before purchasing the animal.

- These animals love playing and running around. These pets are fond of exploring things and can create a mess if not monitored.

Chapter 2: Things to know before you buy a Holland Lop rabbit

Before you buy a Holland Lop rabbit and bring him home to hand raise him, it is important that you understand certain facts regarding these animals. (Please note that although you can have females, we shall refer to them as 'he' for ease). You should understand their behavior and also the cost incurred in domesticating them. Having knowledge of all these things will help you to make a better decision regarding the domestication of the Holland Lop rabbit.

1. Costs that you will incur

It is better that you plan things well in advance. This planning will help you to avoid any kind of disappointment that you might face when there are some payments that need to be made. You should work out all these things right in the beginning, so that you don't suffer any problems later. Realizing at a later stage that you can't keep the animal and giving it up is never a good idea. You can maintain a journal to keep track of the costs.

Cost of the Holland Lop rabbit

The price of the Holland Lop rabbit will depend on where you choose to buy the Holland Lop rabbit from. You can get a rescued rabbit from a rescue centre or animal shelter, if it is available.

The next choice is to buy one from the breeder. The cost will vary depending on the quality of the Holland Lop rabbit. A very good quality Holland Lop rabbit bought from a top class breeder will cost you around $80/£58.06.

Depending on your choice of breeder and the choice of Holland Lop rabbit quality, you can expect to spend $20/£14.52 to $100/£72.58 for buying the bunny.

Health costs

It is important to include the cost of healthcare when working on various costs for the pet Holland Lop. This will help you to get an idea on what you can expect to spend on the general keep of the pet Holland Lop rabbit.

The Holland Lop rabbit does require shots and vaccinations, so you need to spend money on the vaccinations. You can expect to spend $80/£58.06 on both the important vaccines.

The only regular medication that the Holland Lops need is the commercial pellets. These tablets are required to keep the issue of fur block at bay. You can expect to spend about $10/£7.65 on 600 of these tablets. These tablets don't need to be given daily. They can be given twice or thrice a week, so that means 600 tablets will last you a very long time.

You would be relieved to know that the Holland Lop rabbit does not get sick that often. If you take care of the food and hygiene of the bunny, you can save him from many diseases. He will lead a healthy life if you take the necessary precautions.

You should always focus on the health of the Holland Lop rabbit. This is necessary because an unhealthy animal is the breeding ground of many other diseases in the home. Your pet might pass on the diseases to other pets if not treated on time.

The rabbit will not fall sick that often, buy you should bring your pet to the veterinarian for regular check-ups. This is to avoid any future health problems.

You should also be prepared for unexpected costs, such as sudden illness or accident of the Holland Lop rabbit. Health care is provided at different prices in different areas. So, the veterinarian in your area could be costlier than the veterinarian in the nearby town.

Cost of food

A domesticated Holland Lop rabbit will mostly be fed hay, grass and vegetables. You might also have to include various pellets and supplements to give your pet overall nourishment. It is important that you understand the food requirements of your Holland Lop in the beginning, so that you can be prepared on the monetary front.

You should feed about two cups of greens per day to the rabbit. This should cost you around $10/£7.68 per month. You can expect to pay $3/£2.32 to $5/£3.84 for the pellets.

You should make sure that there is enough fibre in the diet of the Holland Lop rabbit. You need to feed timothy hay to the Holland Lop rabbit every day. This should cost you about $3/£2.32 per month.

Cost of hygiene

A pet needs to be clean and hygienic. If you fail at maintaining hygiene levels for your pet, it will only lead to other complications. The basic hygiene of the pet can be maintained by a good quality shampoo and some towels.

There are many owners that insist on litter training. If you too wish to litter train your pet Holland Lop rabbit, you will have to buy the required products for the same. You would need to buy paper litter for the bunny because it is safe even when the rabbit ingests it.

You will also be required to invest in a good detergent, which could be bleach. This will be needed to clean the cage and all the areas where the Holland Lop rabbit might defecate. This is a very basic amount that you will have to encounter. You should invest in some good cleaning products and sanitizers.

You can look at spending $4/£3.07 for the paper litter per month for the pet. The other requirements of shampoo and detergents should not cost you more than $10/£7.66 per month.

Cost of rabbit cage

The shelter of the animal will be his home, so it is important that you construct the shelter according to the animal's needs. If the pet is not indoors, he will probably be in his cage. So, it is important to make this one time investment in a way that is best for the Holland Lop rabbit.

The cage of the Holland Lop rabbit should be six feet long, two feet wide and two feet deep. If you can provide extra space to the Holland Lop, it is better. The price of shelter will depend on the type of the shelter. You can expect to spend $10/£7.66 to $20/£15.36 for the cage.

Miscellaneous costs

Although the main costs that you will encounter while raising your pet have already been discussed, there will be some extra things that you will have to take care of. Most of these are one-time costs only.

You will have to spend money to buy stuff such as grooming comb, litter box, scissors, brush, nail clippers, feed bin, water bottle, accessories and toys for the pet. If you think that something needs to be repaired or replaced, you would have to spend money on doing that.

You can expect to spend some $100/£76.58 on these things. The exact amount will depend on the wear and tear and the quality of the products. In order to keep track of things, you should regularly check the various items in the cage or hutch of the pet bunny.

2. Holland Lop rabbit Vaccination

Your Holland Lop bunnies would need to get vaccinated because almost all breeds of rabbits need vaccination when in captivity to build up their immune system.

It should be noted that vaccination for the Holland Lop bunnies is not available in all countries. You should consult your veterinarian for the latest updates of this. If you are in United Kingdom, it would be easier to get the vaccination done.

The cost of the vaccines will depend on the area you stay. Most of the vets will give a discount as high as 25 per cent if more than one bunny is vaccinated.

Why does the pet bunny need vaccinations?

If you are a new pet parent, you might be in two minds whether the pet animal needs vaccination or not. You should know that there are many reasons to get your pet bunny vaccinated:

- Vaccines allow the bunny to boost up its immunity levels. This could help in preventing various ailments.

- If you want to show your pet in events, vaccination is a requirement to be able to do so.

- If you are aiming at getting rabbit insurance, you would need to get the vaccinations done, otherwise it will be difficult to get the insurance.

- It is also a necessity for rabbit boarding houses.

When and how often should the vaccinations be done?

In a young Holland Lop, the antibody from the mother begins to diminish between the forth and the seventh week. This is when you should aim for the first vaccination.

The bunny should be given the very first vaccine between the sixth and the eighth week. Before the sixth week, the young will be safe because of the maternal immunity. The key here is that this is possible if the mother herself is vaccinated. You will have to get the vaccine shots for the bunny once every year. There is a combined annual vaccine that could be given to the rabbit.

It is important to get the Holland Lop rabbit vaccinated. You should get the bunny vaccinated against myxomatosis and RVHD (Rabbit viral haemorrhagic disease). You will need to give the bunny two vaccines per year to protect him against these two diseases.

If you are in UK, then The Rural land protection act of 1989 makes it compulsory to vaccinate the rabbit with fibroma vaccine. The veterinarian might also advice the caregivers to give the Holland Lop rabbits a vaccine against Calcivirus.

3. Holland Lop rabbit Insurance

You can get insurance for your Holland Lop rabbit. This insurance will help you to take care of the veterinarian bill and injury costs. Though the Holland Lop rabbit does not get sick easily, a sudden procedure can cost you over thousands of pounds and dollars.

If you buy insurance to cover these conditions, you will save yourself from a lot of trouble. Depending on the insurance you buy, you can also cover regular clinic visits. There are some companies that will give you discounts on clinic visits.

There are some companies that can help you with Holland Lop rabbit insurance, such as Exotic direct, pet plan, Helpucover and NCI. These companies have different kinds of insurance. You can choose according to your requirement. You can also get a package deal if you are looking to insure more than one Holland Lop rabbit.

When you buy insurance, you have to pay a deductible amount and regular premiums. You will also be required to pay premiums that need to be paid regularly to keep the insurance policy active.

Rabbit insurance can cost you around $8/£6.14 to $20/£15.35 per month. The exact amount will depend on the company that you choose and also on the area where you live.

4. Neutering or spaying

Neutering or spaying has become an important part of pet domestication. As an owner, you need to make a decision whether you would want your pets to have progenies or not. Holland Lop rabbits can be neutered or spayed by the owners or the breeders. When you are sure that you don't want your doe to breed, it is better to spay the animal before it is too late. Similarly, neuter the male if you don't want breeding.

It should also be understood that neutering or spaying the rabbit will have its consequences on the pet. It is better to understand these consequences. Talk to the veterinarian about them and be prepared for them.

It is known that males get less aggressive if they are neutered at the right age. It is advised to get the process done before it is four months old. If the rabbit is an adult, neutering or spaying will have a lot of complications, which you would definitely want to avoid.

The sexual organs of the rabbits are located towards the inside and they are also very small. The entire process can be very tricky and complicated. It is extremely important that you get the neutering or spaying done by a trained professional who has experience dealing with these animals.

5. Breeding in Holland Lop rabbits

As a new or prospective owner of a Holland Lop rabbit, you might be interested in the breeding cycle and procedure of the Holland Lop rabbits. Breeding is defined as the process of production of an offspring by mating by the male and the female adults. This chapter is meant to clear all your doubts regarding the breeding of Holland Lop rabbits. It is important to understand the breeding patterns of your pet animals. How well you understand the mating patterns of your pet will also determine how well you look after the pet.

There are many owners who are interested in rabbits' breeding and production of the younger ones. The breeding at a controlled environment at your house can be challenging. But, it will get easier to understand once you equip yourself with all the right knowledge.

It is also known that the mother can sometimes kill the kits one after the other. There are many reasons behind this. The mother might do it when she is unable to provide nutrition to the kit.

If the kit has a danger of predators, such as wild dogs, even then the mother might decide to kill the kits. It is important that the mother rabbit is kept under observation during her nesting phase.

If your female rabbit tends to kill its young ones, you will have to keep the little ones away from her. It is known that if the mother kills more than two of her kits, she should not be allowed to breed again.

Mating behaviour of the Holland Lop rabbits

You should understand the natural mating behaviour of your Holland Lops. This will help you to do the right thing while breeding them. This chapter is meant to equip you with all the knowledge that you might need while mating your rabbits.

Each animal species has their unique breeding habits and patterns. When you are looking to take care of your pet well, you should also lay enough emphasis on understanding its breeding patterns.

The male Holland Lop rabbit gets sexually mature at the age of seven to eight months, while the female Holland Lop rabbits get sexually mature a month earlier, which is six to seven months of age.

It should also be noted that the different breeds of Holland Lops differ slightly in the time by which the males and females reach sexual maturity.

The younger Holland Lop rabbits are referred to as bunnies or kits. A male and female Holland Lop is able to produce many kits at a single time. These rabbits are known to be very active sexually. Anyone looking to breed rabbits and produce kits will not be disappointed.

It should be understood that rabbits are able to follow one mating cycle with the other in short durations of times. This means that if the mating procedure of the Holland Lop rabbits is not understood and controlled, your house could be flooded with kits.

A good breeder will always encourage you to thoroughly understand the sexual tendencies of your rabbits, so as to not commit any mistake in the future. You need to know how often and in what conditions your rabbits can reproduce.

In the wild, the kits have higher chances of survival in a warm environment. This means that the rabbits enter their mating cycle in warmer temperatures. You can expect the same when the rabbits are domesticated.

When a rabbit is in its natural environment, the extra amount of light during the summers and also spring brings about a change in its body. The male and female rabbits get sexually active during this time.

A male rabbit will display changes in its behaviour. It will seem more aggressive and restless. This is due to the sex hormones that have become active in its body. This is how you can identify if your male Holland Lop is ready to mate or not.

Another interesting behaviour that can be noted in the males is that they become more competitive with other male rabbits. The males who are sexually active compete with each other to establish dominance in the group. This is done so that they can impress the female and attract her for mating.

It is known that in the wild, the dominant male Holland Lops have a good sex life in comparison to the shy ones. When you see your pet male Holland Lop getting too aggressive and competitive, you should know that he is ready for mating.

When your male rabbit and female rabbit are ready for mating, you should bring the female rabbit to the male rabbit's cage. It should be noted that the opposite should not be done.

You should not take the male rabbit to the female rabbit's cage because the female rabbit can get territorial. You might find the female attacking and harming the male instead of mating with him.

Once the male rabbit (buck) is able to attract the female rabbit (doe), the mating can begin. During the process, the female will lie down on a level surface on the ground as an invitation to the male rabbit. The female will also lift its tail.

The male will mount himself on the female rabbit at this time. The male is known to cast a sharp bite on the nape of the female at this time. This process should last over twenty seconds.

The mating process will end here and the male will release the female at this time. It should also be noted that the male rabbit will have fur in his mouth because of the bite he had cast. He will also lose his consciousness for some time after the entire process is over.

Now, the female is pregnant. The gestation period in the female will last for over a month. Once that is over, you can expect your pregnant Holland Lop to give birth to three to eight kits or bunnies.

It should be noted that the new born kits are hairless. They are also blind at this time. The female is capable of repeating the same process and giving birth to bunnies many times in a year.

6. Purchasing a Holland Lop rabbit

Once you have made up your mind whether you want to buy the Holland Lop rabbit or not, the next obvious step is to look for the right place to buy it. You can do so from a pet store or directly from a breeder.

Before you buy your Holland Lop rabbit, it is important that you do your research well. You should also have the right information about various pet stores and breeders in your area.

You can visit various pet stores to look for the kind of Holland Lop rabbit that you are looking for. The local veterinarian can give his/her recommendations in this case. It is always advisable to buy a Holland Lop rabbit from a reputable breeder.

The problem with pet stores is that you would not come to know about the history of the rabbit, which is so important to understand the health of the animal. You will also not be able to understand the breeding process and conditions of the animal. These are some important factors in determining the health and the history of the animal.

Buying a rabbit from a breeder has many benefits. You can talk to the breeder about the many concerns that you might have. You can understand the breeding procedure of the animal and can also be sure that the animal has been in safe hands before you.

You should also make sure that you select the right breeder to buy the rabbit from. It is as important as buying the right pet. If you choose the wrong breeder, you will only have to face problems in the future.

It will pay to talk to other people who have bought rabbits in your region. They could help you in deciding on the right breeders.

There are some breeders who are in this profession for the love of Holland Lop rabbits and animals in general. Of course they wish to earn money, but not by compromising their prime duty as a breeder.

You will also find breeders who do this only for the sake of money. Such breeders will not hesitate in providing you with the wrong information about the rabbit to make a few bucks. You need to save yourself from such selfish breeders.

It is important that you devote some time in looking for breeders in and around your region. You should understand the reputation of the breeder before you choose him/her to buy your rabbit from.

As the potential buyer, you should know every little detail about your pet animal. You need to make sure that the breeder you choose to buy the Holland Lop rabbit from shares all the details about the rabbit.

A good breeder will always ask you questions and will make sure that the animal will get a good owner and a good home. You can expect this from a breeder who cares enough for the animals that he/she keeps.

The breeder would want to understand the prime motive behind you buying the rabbit. He/she would also want to understand if you have the time and energy to devote to the rabbit. The Holland Lop rabbit can be demanding as a pet, and you should make sure that you can provide for it.

There have been cases where the breeders have denied permission to the prospective owners because they didn't seem able to provide well for the animal. So if your breeder is asking you questions about how you intend to keep the animal, then this is a good sign.

The breeder will also give you a set of instructions that will come in handy when you are taking care of the rabbit. You should make sure that you understand these instructions well.

List of rescue websites

You also have the option of adopting a rabbit. There are some factors that will govern the final choice that you make. You should make sure that you understand these factors, so that you can make the right choice for yourself as the owner of a new pet.

Many rabbits are mistreated and abandoned by their owners. You can help to give one of these abandoned rabbits a new home. The abandoned rabbit will get a new home and your family will get a new pet.

If you want to buy a kit or younger rabbit, then you should buy him from a good breeder. If you are looking to bring an older rabbit to your home, then you should try to go for adoption.

If you are looking at the financial side of the deal, then you can benefit from adopting the rabbit. Many a times, you can expect to get a cage and other accessories with the abandoned rabbit. This will save you from building or buying a new cage for the animal.

Most adult Holland Lop rabbits are vaccinated and litter trained. They are also spayed or neutered. This will also help you to save some money.

If you are looking for reputed breeders, then the following list can help you:

- Rabbit haven: https://therabbithaven.org
- Bunnies are us: www.bunniesareus.com
- Dwarf R US: www.dwarfsrus.com
- Rabbit breeders: http://rabbitbreeders.us
- Evergreen farm: www.evergreenfarm.biz
- Friends of rabbits: www.friendsofrabbits.org

7. Licensing requirements

Once you are acquainted with the basic knowledge about the Holland Lop rabbits, the next important question is whether a license is needed to domesticate them. Before you can decide from where you should buy the bunny, it is important to know about the licensing requirements.

It is important to understand the licensing rules of the Holland Lop rabbits. You should be sure that the laws permit you to hand raise the animal. This is important because the law prohibits the domestication of certain animals.

When you are planning to domesticate the Holland Lop rabbits, you should understand the licensing laws properly. This would help you to avoid future hassles with the law.

Make sure that you understand all the laws that govern the domestication of the pet. You would definitely want to save yourself from any future trouble.

You should understand each detail before you go and buy the Holland Lop rabbit. In case you domesticate an animal against the law, the penalty could even include seizure of the animal.

It is important that you understand that the steps of obtaining the license would essentially be the same in most places, there could be slight variations between the various regions.

Different regions would have their own regulations. This makes it essential for you to contact the local council of your region.

Licensing in the United States

If you live in the United States of America, then you should know that there is no federal law governing the domestication of the Holland Lop rabbit. This means that you don't need a license in the United States of America.

Though there is no law that will prohibit you from keeping these rabbits, there are certain state laws that govern the keeping and also breeding of these animals. It is important to understand these state laws, so that you don't violate the law.

It should be noted that certain areas require you to have a permit or license. Minnesota requires a person to acquire a permit at $15/£11.37 per year if he/she wishes to domesticate a Holland Lop rabbit. If the Holland Lop rabbit is not spayed or neutered, you can expect to pay even more.

A retail pet store owner does not require a permit or license to keep the Holland Lop rabbits. It should also be noted that private rabbit collectors also don't need a license. But, if they plan to breed the rabbits, the laws will vary.

Licensing in United Kingdom

If you reside in the United Kingdom, then you should know that there is no legal law that governs the keeping of Holland Lop rabbits. There are certain people who collect and breed these bunnies for exhibitions or wholesale benefits. If you belong to this category, even then you don't have to obtain a permit or license from the state.

Though needing and keeping of the Holland Lops is easy, the import and export of Holland Lop bunnies will require a permit. There is a license called AML, the Animal Movement License, which is required by a person trying to import or export a bunny from the United Kingdom.

8. Holland Lop rabbits and other pets

If you are keen on domesticating Holland Lop rabbits with other pet animals, then it is important that you understand the temperament of the various animals.

Holland Lop rabbits and other rabbits

If you are planning on keeping more than one Holland Lop rabbit, you should understand their behavioral and spatial requirements. If you already have a rabbit and are planning to buy more, you need to make sure that the pets can live together happily.

One of the most important criteria that needs to be kept in mind is the space that you would provide the rabbits. The animals need the right amount of space to grow and develop.

These animals are known to be very active. You should be able to provide them a space where they can hop around without any constraints. There should be enough space for all the pets. If an animal has to compete with other animals for space, it will only lead to more trouble in the future.

The rabbits can get territorial and can fight with each other to establish their territory. You will have to keep a check on the pets to understand their basic behavior and their urge to establish a territory.

The rabbits can also grow fond of each other and live peacefully. Things will basically come down to the individual temperaments of the animals. You will have to devote some time to understanding it.

The age of the rabbits is another factor that should be taken into account. It is also known that if the rabbits are introduced to each other at a very young age, there is a chance that they will get along well.

It should be noted that you can keep a Holland Lop rabbit with other breeds of rabbits also, as long as there is space for everybody. An ideal scenario would be where you keep two to three rabbits. Remember to buy them at a young age so that they can grow together and bond well.

If you are looking to domesticate more than one Holland Lop rabbit, it is advised that you keep pairs of brothers and sisters. They will get along well. You can also keep pairs of males and females. As a rule, there should not be more than one male rabbit for two female rabbits.

Holland Lop rabbits and other pets

Holland Lop rabbits are social and loveable animals. You can expect your Holland Lop rabbit to be friendly towards other pets, but you will have to make sure that the pets are comfortable with each other.

If your Holland Lop rabbit is very young, you should make sure that you save him from bigger animals in the house that have a high prey drive. For example, a big cat might try to hunt the poor rabbit.

These animals might try to hurt the rabbit, and he would be too young to protect himself from any danger coming his way.

The type of pet is a very important criterion while determining whether the pets will get along or not. The Holland Lop rabbit will definitely get along with another sociable and friendly pet. If it finds the other animal a threat, then they will not get along.

If you are very keen on keeping more than one kind of pet in the household, then it is better that the Holland Lop rabbit and the other pets are made to socialize right from a young age. This will help them to bond well with each other.

The less the space for the animals, the more difficult it will get for you to raise your pets. So, space is one factor that will always be important when you are hand raising your pets. You should always keep this in mind.

No matter how things are looking, you should always keep a close eye on your pets. Never commit the mistake of leaving them on their own. You might not realize but they can harm each other. The first few interactions need to be all the more monitored.

If you notice your pets are not getting along well with each other, it is important that you don't force them to interact. They should be allowed to interact and bond in a very natural way. In the case where the pets can't get along even after multiple tries, you should keep them away from each other so that no one is harmed in any way.

Chapter 3: Handling a Holland Lop rabbit

When you are a pet parent, one of your greatest concerns would be how to handle the pet. What should you do? What shouldn't you do?

If you have a Holland Lop rabbit or are planning to get one, you should be very careful about how you handle the pet. Any wrong signal from your side and your pet can panic.

A rabbit is said to be a prey animal. In the wild, it is preyed on by many stronger animals such as snakes. A new touch sets them into a panic mode.

The first few times when you approach the Holland Lop bunny, you need to be extra careful. Don't do anything that can scare the animal. Take it slow and give the pet animal some time.

Don't expect the Holland Lop to love you the very first time you pick him up. With time, the pet will learn that when you pick him up, its mean something good.

This chapter will teach you everything that you need to know about handling the Holland Lop rabbit.

1. How to relax the bunny?

When you first approach the bunny, don't just take him in your arms. This might shock the pet. Take it slow. You need to relax the Holland Lop.

Massaging is a technique that can help you to relax the animal. Your touch will also help you to create a bond with him. This might be a slow process, but it will be a steady one.

A good massage helps the pet to release tension, pain and inflammation. It also increases the range of the motion.

The pet can get help with any behavioural issues that it might be having. Massage also strengthens immunity, improves circulation and accelerates recovery.

You should slowly massage the Holland Lop rabbit from the head to the toes. Keep your hands gentle and make use of your fingers.

Notice the reactions of the Holland Lop rabbits. This will help you to decide what changes you want to incorporate while handling the pet.

Handling a nervous rabbit

When a Holland Lop rabbit moves into your house, he will be very nervous. This is a very normal behaviour, so don't be surprised. You should work harder on handling a nervous Holland Lop bunny.

It is important to make him feel comfortable and a part of the family. This is a process that will take some time. Don't expect the rabbit to start dancing with you the first time he sees you.

2. How to pick up the rabbit?

While you might love the idea of a small and cuddly pet that you can lift in your arms, you need to be very careful.

You don't want to scare the pet. It is important to establish a trust factor with the pet Holland Lop bunny.

This section will help you to understand how you should pick up your rabbit. The right knowledge will give you the confidence to do it in the right way.

Use both your hands while picking up the bunny. Don't attempt to pick him up with one hand. You might accidentally hurt the Holland Lop rabbit.

Use one hand to support to bottom of the Holland Lop bunny. Use the other hand to give support to the chest of the bunny. You can keep the thumb over the bunny's shoulder to give it a better grip.

The Holland Lop bunny might try to jump out of your grip. You need to be careful with this. Make sure you are gentle yet firm in your grip.

The position of the bunny rabbit should be such that the head should be held higher in comparison to the bottom. The bottom of the bunny rabbit needs to be tucked inwards.

It should be noted here that in this particular stance you should only move the rabbit for shorter distances. Don't take him on the road for a walk.

If you have to travel longer distances, you should keep the bunny as close to your chest as possible. This will keep the bunny warm and safe. He will also not be able to get out of your grip.

Everything that you attempt with your bunny should be done slowly. The first time just lift him up and leave him.

The next time, you can hold him for a little longer. In this way, the bunny would also be able to recognise you and the entire process will become very easy.

3. Carrying your rabbit

When you learn to pick up your bunny in the right way, the initial few times you should only move a few steps in your house.

When you are confident that you can hold the pet well, you should carry him for longer distances.

Using a rabbit carrier

If you are confused about how you can make good use of a rabbit carrier then this section will help you to do it. You will learn how you can use the rabbit carrier in an easy and effective way.

A rabbit carrier can be defined as a pet case. This pet case has a side, front or top doors. These doors are used for moving the pet inside or outside the pet case.

You should prefer a rabbit case that has a top opening. Your second choice should be the one that has a side door.

Using a pet carrier or not would be your personal choice. There are some pet parents that don't need to use it.

On the other hand, there are some pet parents that use it, especially when they are new at handling their Holland Lop rabbits.

A rabbit carrier can help you gain some confidence when you are a novice with the bunny. It will also keep the pet safe, without you having to worry too much.

Firstly, you should acquaint the pet carrier to the pet bunny. If you suddenly try to put him in then he might resist.

For a couple of days, before you plan to put the bunny in it, keep it in the vicinity of the Holland Lop bunny. You can keep the door open so that the pet feels welcome to go and sit in it.

If the pet is not showing much interest then you can make use of some simple tricks. You can keep your bunny's favourite treat in the carrier. This will attract him towards it.

You should keep some hay inside the pet carrier. This will avoid any mishaps. The pet can get all excited and might slip. The hay will prevent any such event.

If the carrier has a side door, the pet will easily get in. If the door is on the top then help the bunny to get in if he does not hop in.

When you use the pet carrier to transport the pet in a car, you should make sure that the carrier is balanced in the car. If it is not balanced, the bunny could get severe injuries.

You should also maintain good air flow in the car. The poor bunny will have a hard time in the pet carrier if the flow of air is not good.

4. What is the right way to put your rabbit down?

When we talk about rabbit handling, we are not just referring to picking him up and carrying him around. You also need to put the rabbit down in the correct way.

These steps might seem very simple and mundane to many people, but they actually form the core of a good a relationship you can form with your bunny.

If you can't pick a rabbit well or carry him well or put him down in the correct way, what can you expect from the bunny?

Any lapse from your side will have a direct effect on your beloved bunny. If you fail to handle him delicately, he will start getting scared of you. He will hesitate to come to you. The bond between you two will be destroyed even before it is formed.

Assuming that you have learnt to pick-up your rabbit well and carry him around well, this section will focus on how to put him down.

Firstly, you have to be careful while putting the bunny back in his house or on the ground. The bunny can be very unpredictable. One minute, he'll be siting calmly in your hands and the next minute, he will try to jump out.

So, don't assume that the pet will not try to jump from your grip. This is very much possible. You should hold the grip till the bunny is on the ground.

Some bunnies have the habit of kicking backwards when they get free from a grip. You need to watch out for this behaviour in the pet.

As the bunny goes down, he will recognise his hutch or house and might get excited. You need to make sure that he stays calm.

You should make sure that the pet Holland Lop rabbit does not hurt you or does not hurt himself while kicking backwards.

5. Gaining the trust of the pet bunny

Gaining trust of your bunny is one of your first challenges when you deal with the pet. He will take his own time and you have to allow him that time.

It is not an overnight or one day process. It is a process that is slow but when done in the right way can give you very fruitful results.

It is important to enjoy the process. This should be a special time in your life and also your pet's life.

If you are worried about gaining the trust of your pet then you don't need to worry anymore. This section will help you to understand how you can gain the trust of your Holland Lop bunny.

Give them time to observe you

You might not realise but your pet bunny will always have his eyes on you. He will quietly try to understand you and things related to you.

Some people believe that sitting next to the bunny all the time when he is new will help the bunny. But in reality, you should allow some down time for the pet.

Don't leave him all alone. Keep him in the vicinity. But, don't sit at his feet at all times. You should go about your day in a normal fashion.

The pet Holland Lop rabbit will keep a close eye on your routine. Make sure that the bunny is placed at a comfortable spot, preferably in a cage so that it can't run away.

A Holland Lop rabbit can get bored very easily. Being at a spot in the house where he can observe you and also the other house mates will keep him entertained. He will also get to know your family in a better way.

Sit quietly with the rabbit

Every day when you have some time at your disposal, sit next to your bunny. Don't pet him or hug him. Just sit next to him.

You can cuddle him, massage him or play with him when he gets used to you. But, there has to be a few minutes when you do absolutely nothing with him.

You can keep 20-30 minutes aside. Sit near the rabbit and watch him. You will notice that as the days pass, the pet will start recognising you. He will slowly start coming to you.

Don't touch him till he is comfortable

This is a simple rule that you need to follow. You can cuddle him, massage him or play with him at a later stage when he gets used to you. You will have ample time to do all that with the rabbit.

The Holland Lop can get very nervous if you try to touch him all the time. This simply means that he still does not know you. You should give hime more time.

Feeding

During the initial days, you have to be careful with him while serving food also. Remember not to touch him.

Just keep the food next to him. He will eat on his own. If you force him, he will develop a strong disliking for you.

Give the bunny treats

Treats go a long way in making the pet happy. He will get very excited when you offer him a treat.

You will take time to figure out his favourite foods, so serve him treats generally enjoyed by all rabbits such as carrots.

Make sure that you don't give anything sugary or unhealthy to speed up the bonding process with the pet Holland Lop rabbit.

Light petting

Slowly, the Holland Lop rabbit will get used to you being around. He will start getting comfortable with you. You can slowly start touching him and petting him.

You will see that he will start recognising you. He will also get used to your smell. You should definitely not get over excited here.

Take the process slow. Start with light petting. Let the Holland Lop bunny play outside in the open space of your house. Be around him at this time.

You should always start by brushing the head area of the pet bunny. If you think that the pet does not like it, stop it.

The best areas to pet the Holland Lop rabbit are the forehead, the shoulders and behind the ears. They might not like you petting under the head area and at the back end.

Regular interaction

You have to be consistent and persistent. This is the only way you can make a good bond between your cute bunny and you.

Don't give up when things seem rough. Just understand what you might be doing wrong and then correct it.

Slowly you can start talking to the pet while you are petting him. This will help you to form a stronger bond with the Holland Lop rabbit.

Chapter 4: Habitat requirements

Pets require a proper shelter so that you can keep them safe from the changes in weather and also from possible attacks from predators. It is advisable that you make the necessary arrangements for your pet before you bring him home so that you can get him straight into his shelter when he is home.

Most rabbits, if given a choice, would love to spend all their time outside. They love free spaces where they can play and be merry.

While a rabbit might enjoy his time outside in the open, he will also love to stay indoors. He would enjoy the familiarity and warmth of the indoor spaces. It gives them a feeling for being in their burrows.

This is one debate that a rabbit parent is also having in his head, whether to keep the bunny inside or to make arrangements to let him spend most of his time outside.

The key here is to balance things. Each pet animal is an individual. He would be different from any other animal. This makes it important that you understand the unique temperament of your pet.

You should make arrangements so that the pet bunny can be kept both indoors and outdoors. This will be an ideal situation for the rabbit. Of course, you can only plan according to the space that your house permits.

If you are a rabbit enthusiast then you should do the best you can do for the habitat and housing of your pet animal. This chapter will help you to plan well.

1. Rabbit house guidelines

If you are planning on keeping Holland Lop rabbits or already have them at your home, there are a few guidelines that you need to take care of.

These guidelines will ensure that you give the right environment to the Holland Lop rabbit where he can grow and flourish.

The law

It is also important to understand what the law says in regard to the keeping and housing of the bunny rabbits.

The Animal Welfare Act of 2006 directs all rabbit owners to meet all the welfare needs of the pet rabbit. You are expected to provide a suitable environment where the pet can grow.

When we talk about providing a suitable environment for growth, we are basically talking about diet, health, company, behaviour and housing of the pet animal.

How much space would the bunny rabbit need?

This is the first question that pops in the minds of people that are interested in keeping bunny rabbits. Many people feel that a rabbit is so small so he can be kept in a small shoe box or something similar.

It doesn't work like this. Just because the pet is small does not mean that he does not need space of his own. You have to have a hutch or cage for the rabbit that is at least six feet in length.

If you are wondering as to why the bunny needs so much space then you need to know that the rabbit needs to hop around and run. A bunny that is not able to do so will only get depressed.

You will have to take the depressed and sick bunny to the veterinarian. This will cost you lots of extra effort and bucks.

So, to save yourself from any future discomfort, you should invest in a good housing scheme for the rabbit. Make sure that whatever you decide allows the rabbit to sit, eat and roam around freely. He should not feel restricted in any way.

A normal sized rabbit will take 2-3 feet of space when it is stretching. The same will take 3-4 feet height when it is standing. A hop can be of a length of 6-7 feet.

Never go by the size of the rabbit to decide its hutch size. A small rabbit can be very energetic and might need more space than a bigger one. The criteria should be the personality of the rabbit that you plan to keep.

Keeping in mind the personality of the Holland Lop bunny, you should invest in a hutch that is 3 by 7 feet in dimension. The house of the rabbit should allow it to hop 3 to 4 times in one go.

Space required by multiple rabbits

If you are planning on keeping more than one bunny then you need to be careful about a few things. You can't expect the hutch for one Holland Lop rabbit to be ideal for more than one rabbit.

You need more space for multiple rabbits. It is as simple as that. The rabbits need space to move around. They will start falling sick if space restricts them in any way. This is the last thing that a pet parent would want for his beautiful bunnies.

2. Rabbit hutch

A rabbit hutch can be defined as a cage for the rabbit that is constructed generally with wood and a wire mesh that surrounds it. Most rabbit hutches have long legs to keep them anywhere. The ones without legs can be placed over tables or other safe surfaces.

Building a rabbit hutch is one of the most popular choices. You should make sure that you have the provisions to build it in your house. You can keep one in the backyard, basement or any other area of the house.

It is important that you understand that a rabbit hutch is only one option that you have when your pet needs to be kept in a cage like environment. This does not mean that you keep the pet in the hutch and forget about him.

The hutch needs to be easily accessible to you or a family member. You should check on the rabbit from time to time. You should also allow the pet some time outside the hutch to just walk around.

Many cases have been reported in the past where the owners' negligence towards the Holland Lop rabbits caused serious issues in the animals, such as stress and depression. You can't abandon your rabbit in a comfortable hutch.

The pet should be kept indoors as much as possible. The hutch can be used when you are not around to care for the pet.

You can buy the rabbit hutch or can design it yourself. It is important that it meets all the requirements of the pet animal. To begin with, the hutch needs to be spacious. The animal should have enough space to walk around.

You should make sure that the rabbit hutch does not suffocate the rabbit. It should be airy and well ventilated. You should make sure that the rabbit has access to food and water in the rabbit hutch. You can install a feed hopper and a good watering system in the rabbit hutch to ensure the same.

You should also try to make the hutch attractive for the rabbit. He should not feel bored and suffocated in there. The hutch should feel like a fun home for him. There are some simple ways in which you can make the hutch a lively place for the rabbit.

Keep some small and interesting toys for the Holland Lop rabbit in the hutch. You should make sure that the toys don't scare the pet away. They should be inviting and fun for him. This will keep him happy and entertained.

The rabbit hutch should allow proper sanitation. Many cases of diseases have been reported in Holland Lop rabbits due to improper sanitation.

The rabbit's hutch would need to be cleaned regularly to make sure that there are no disease carrying bacteria and viruses in there. These are simple things, but critical when it comes to the wellbeing of the pet in the long run.

The nest boxes that are used for the kits should be sanitized regularly. They should be stored safely and properly when not in use. You can store them and use them for the next set of kits that you might have.

If you are planning to keep more than one Holland Lop rabbit, then you can work on giving them a common habitat. Some people would choose to give separate shelters to the animals. The idea of providing separate shelters is also fine.

If the pets get along, then they can be kept in a common cage. However, in case the rabbits are not getting along, keeping them in a common cage will only lead to more problems in the future, so this should be avoided.

If you are planning on domesticating more than one rabbit, you can consider buying another cage. This cage could be very simple and basic. The main purpose of this extra cage is to use it when one of the rabbits is sick. The cage will help you to isolate the sick pet animal.

A vet will always advise you to isolate a sick pet. This is necessary so that the pet can recover nicely in the absence of other pets. He would need some space to himself. What is also important is that he should not transmit the disease to the healthy pets. The isolation helps to avoid such a situation.

Precautions with an outdoor hutch

If you are planning to keep an outdoor hutch, there are a few precautions that you would have you would have to take. These simple steps and precautions will ensure that the pet bunny is happy and safe in an outdoor enclosure.

Firstly, the outdoor hutch needs to be kept in a shady area. If the place gets too hot for the rabbit, it can lead to stress in the animal. This is especially important in summers and if you live in a place that is mostly hot.

The outdoor enclosure needs to be kept in a way that you can be sure that all predators are away from the hutch. You could be busy inside the house while some predator might attack and even kill the poor Holland Lop rabbit.

The Holland Lop rabbit is very small in size. This makes it an easy prey for some ferocious animals such as the fox, dog and cat. It is important to take the right measures to save the Holland Lop rabbit from these dangerous and ferocious predators.

Positioning of the rabbit hutch or rabbit house

This might be surprising for many people out there but the truth is that the positioning of the rabbit hutch will also have an effect on the Holland Lop rabbit.

You should understand that wild rabbits are used to surviving in different kinds of climate. But, protection against extreme cold or extreme hot weather and rains would need to be provided.

This section will help you decide the positioning of the rabbit hutch according to various important factors and guidelines.

A hutch facing the north will subject the bunny to the worst of bad climate. A hutch facing the east will help the bunny to face the rising sun.

A hutch facing the south will subject the bunny to the sunshine during sunny days. A hutch facing the west will make the bunny face the setting sun.

Facing the weather conditions

The weather of your country will also have an effect on the Holland Lop rabbit. This section will help you to understand how to construct the rabbit home keeping the weather conditions in mind.

You should understand that wild rabbits are used to surviving in different kinds of climates. But, protection against extreme cold or extreme hot weather and rains would need to be provided.

If the weather is too cold, it is recommended that the protection of the rabbit hutch is increased. Over the top of the hutch, you add a sheet that provided added protection.

You can also move the hutch to a safer place. If you can't keep it inside, then an outhouse or garage will do. Make sure there are no exhaust fumes in these areas, especially car garages. This can be detrimental to the pet bunny's health.

You can also keep the rabbit hutch in a porch that is shaded well. This will provide some relief to the rabbit.

The point that needs to be noted here is that in the intention to keep the rabbit warm, don't make the environment too hot. This will add to the trouble of the Holland Lop rabbit. If you have heat radiators in the home or porch, you need to take care of this point.

A rabbit that is accustomed to live outside will grow a thick undercoat. This helps him to bear the winters. So, make sure that you make them comfortable but don't overheat them.

While care is taken during the cold weather, appropriate measures should also be taken during extreme hot weather. First and foremost, the house of the rabbit should be properly ventilated.

You can also open the roof for some time of you feel that the air flow in the bunny's hutch is not good enough.

If possible, keep the bunny hutch in an elevated area. You can keep it on bricks or something more convenient. Keep the hutch in a shady area during the day time.

You should keep the hutch in a place where there is no direct sunlight. This will help the bunny to save itself from a heatstroke. Also, make sure that there is water available for the Holland Lop rabbit at all times.

You should also protect the bunny hutch from rain. It is known that a Holland Lop bunny's coat takes a lot of time to dry. So, getting wet in the rain is not a good option.

The Holland Lop rabbit might just fall sick because of the rain water. While the rain is pouring, the bunny would not be able to keep itself warm. This means an invitation to illness.

If a strong wind is blowing along with the rain, it is even worse for the Holland Lop rabbit. The safety of the Holland Lop rabbit is in your hands. Make sure that you keep the bunny hutch in a safe and secure place where the rain drops can't reach him.

3. Rabbit hutch alternatives

You can always invest in a traditional rabbit hutch type, but if you are looking for options then you'll be happy to know that you have many.

There are many people that creatively transform a big chicken house into a rabbit house. If you have a chicken house lying around unused, you can do this too.

You can also transform an old garden shed or a child's playhouse that is no longer in use into a fully functional rabbit house.

Barrels made of solid oak can be procured from a local brewery. They can be transformed into beautiful looking rabbit houses.

You can construct a protected rabbit enclosure for your Holland Lop bunny. This is especially good for people that live in areas that are frequented by many potential predators of the bunny.

You can construct a house for your bunny with the help of bamboos in your garden. Bamboo allows flow of air and also protects from rain.

If you have lots of space in your garden area, you can invest in huge sand pits. This can be fun if you have more than one bunny. They will love digging, playing, moulding and resting in the sand beds.

Handmade rabbit housing

There are many big retailers that have bestselling rabbit hutches. You can always choose to buy them. On the other hand, you can also choose handmade rabbit housing.

If you talk to other pet parents in your area or look around, you might find some good small scale craftsmen that will make a rabbit house according to your guidelines.

You can get a bigger hutch made for the same price as you would have spent in buying a hutch from a big retailer.

Indoor rabbit housing

If you have enough space in the your house, then indoor housing should definitely be considered. Rabbits love being indoors as much as they love being outdoors.

The bunnies are very easy to get along with. You and your family can easily share a home with the Holland Lop rabbit. The bunny can also get along well with other pets in the house such as cats and dogs.

Rabbits love warm spaces. They love their corners and take pride in them. They love being with the family.

If your pet spends a lot of time indoors. it is also an opportunity for you to get to know the pet animal better. The pet will keep the family happy and entertained. This will also allow you to form a close bond with the Holland Lop rabbit.

The bunny will not be very difficult to handle. It will learn your schedule and his schedule very quickly. He will know when he can expect food and what is expected from him.

A bunny remembers things. He remembers faces of people and their smells. They don't hold grudges for long even if something upsets them. They can be a treat to live with.

4. Accessories

When you bring a pet home, the pet will be scared of the new surroundings. You will have to make all the attempts that will help the pet to adjust in the new environment.

When you are planning the furnishing and accessories of the shelter, you should make sure that you give the pet an environment that closely resembles his natural habitat. This will keep him happy and spirited.

Besides the basic stuff such as food and water, it is also important to accessorize the cage well. This is important because the right accessories will help him to feel like he is at home. They will bring him closer to his natural habitat and natural tendencies.

There are several accessories available these days that will help you to keep your pet happy. If you go to a pet shop, you will get many ideas for the accessories that you can keep in the cage of the pet.

Bedding

Keeping your pets warm is very important. For this, adequate bedding material is necessary. This not only provides warmth but also protects the animal against any chance of injury. When the Holland Lop rabbit lies down on the floor, he will be comfortable with good bedding.

The bedding material should be free from mold and too much dust. The material should also be non-toxic to a Holland Lop rabbit. The best option is matting, as it is also absorbent by nature.

You can even add material like straw, shavings and other material that can absorb any urine. This should be changed regularly and be well managed to ensure complete hygiene and disease prevention.

There are many types of bedding available these days that can help your pet to have rest and fun when he wants. For example, you can get bedding in the shape of a cave. This will be fun for the pet. The right kind of bedding provided for the rabbit is a simple way of keeping the pet animal comfortable and stress-free.

There are cage liners easily available on the market. You can use these to line the bottom of the cage. They are easy to attach and detach, so are very popular amongst owners.

It is also important that the cage is deep for this type of setting. The liners should be made from a good quality fabric. These liners are safe for the pet because they don't have sharp pieces that can hurt him.

It is easier for the pet to walk on these liners. Fabric liners are actually considered the best option for a bunny's cage. One disadvantage of these liners would be that the pet will try to dig into them and might also spill his food and water. It can be inconvenient to the pet-parent at such a time.

Another popular choice of bedding for the cage is wood shavings. It is important that the shavings are free from phenol. It is also important that the cage is deep, otherwise the shavings will just fall off.

The pet can safely dig in these wood shavings. He can have his fun in this simple way. The wood shavings are relatively odorless because they allow air amongst the shavings.

The wood shavings also have some disadvantages. The shavings will keep falling in the eyes of the pet or they might fall in the water or food containers.

You can use aspen shavings. They are considered the safest of all. The second choice of shavings could be kiln dried pine shavings. You should not use untreated pine shavings or cedar shavings. These can be harmful for the pet.

If you can't install liners in the cage of the Holland Lop rabbit, then paper shavings is your second best option. They look quite similar to the wood shavings.

One downside of this kind of bedding is that the paper bedding is very dusty in nature. This might lead to dry skin in your Holland Lop rabbit. If your pet already has dry skin, the condition might be aggravated.

Rugs and blankets

You can also keep a couple of warm blankets inside the cage. The bunny will play and will also bite them. The rabbit will also like snuggling into the blanket. You should try to make the cage as comfortable as possible, so that the pet animal does not feel like a captive and starts liking the cage.

If the Holland Lop rabbit is old, clipped or is injured, you have to keep him protected from any draft or low temperature. You can also use these rugs to keep flies at bay. Any turnout rug should be removed in case the weather improves to prevent the cage from getting very warm.

The size of the rug should be good enough to suit the size of the bunny. You need the right size to ensure that there are no abrasions, hair loss or restricted movements. They should be removed on a regular basis to check the body condition of the pet. You should also make sure that the bunny does not get too hot because of the rug being on him constantly.

The rugs should be cleaned and repaired regularly. In case of any wetness in the rugs, you should have a spare one that you can use on your pet animal. These precautions ensure that the animal stays clear of any illnesses.

Containers for food and water

It is also extremely important that you give due importance to the containers that would be used to serve food and water to the Holland Lop rabbits. What makes this important is the fact that dirty containers are carriers of allergies and diseases. These allergies and diseases can further turn into serious issues if not treated well.

The containers should also be sturdy enough to hold all the food and water. They should also allow the pet to feed himself without any difficulty. So, even if you have not thought of selecting containers as an important step in animal care, you can do so now.

The food containers should be of good quality and should ideally be made of aluminum or good grade plastic. A poor quality container will only contribute towards spoiling the food, which is something you will never want. The spoilt food is not just a hassle for you, but is also harmful to the health of your bunny.

A water container has some limitations. It can lead to wet coat for the rabbit, which in turn can lead to many water borne diseases. You can use specialized water bottles to keep water for the rabbit in the cage.

If you are concerned about the soiling of the food or if you have more than one pet that would eat from the same food container, then a hayrack could be your ideal buy. A trough or pellet bin with hayracks will help you to avoid the soiling of food items.

The container would also allow more than one animal to eat from the same container. You should choose a size that is most ideal for you. Each animal should get enough space to eat comfortably.

The containers should be washed with good quality soap powder at least twice a week. It is very important that the containers are kept clean at all times. Do not forget to remove the leftover food or dirty water from the containers.

There are many different kinds of feeders available today. You should go for a feeder that suits your needs the best.

5. Blocking off dangerous areas

There is no use crying after the damage has been done. It is always better to take the necessary precautions in the very beginning. You should understand the various tendencies of the Holland Lop rabbit that can pose harm to him.

It is always a good idea to block off dangerous areas. This will mean that the Holland Lop rabbit will not be able to enter these areas, and you will be able to avoid any kind of mishaps.

You can use barriers to make sure that the Holland Lop rabbit can't reach certain spots and rooms in the house. But, a point that needs to be noted here is that good quality barriers will have to be used.

You should know that a Holland Lop rabbit can jump a long distance. So, blocking off areas should be done keeping this in mind. While they can easily jump off bookshelves, they can also squeeze behind one.

Puppy pens and baby gates are two options that you can consider while you are looking for ways to block off certain areas of the house. You can easily find them online or from a store.

Make sure that you make a list of all the areas in the house that you want to block from the bunny. You can choose to block a complete room or certain sections. You should know where you don't want your pet.

It is a good idea to make sure that the barriers are made of good quality metal. This will ensure that the bunny can't chew on it. The last thing that you would want is the Holland Lop chewing off the barriers that were meant to block him.

You should make sure that the right kinds of barriers are used. This is because your naughty Holland Lop rabbit will happily climb small barriers. He might even get his head stuck in the barrier openings, inviting more trouble for himself and for you also.

If you don't want to invest in high end barriers, then you can look for cheaper alternatives. You can find different kinds of barriers online. Or, you could get these barriers from a shop. They will help to solve your purpose and will be easier on your pocket.

These barriers have a very strong base of plastic. The plastic is good quality and also non-toxic. Barriers made of Plexiglas will also serve the purpose right.

You can make safe and secure barriers on your own. If you wish to make the barrier at your home, then you can use wood. Make sure that you understand how you need to make them.

You can also take some measures to keep the pet bunny away from your furniture. This is important so that they don't try to create a tunnel by chewing on the fabric.

You can also use a good piece of cardboard as a barrier. You can fix some heavy material of cardboard at the bottom end of the furniture that you are trying to protect. This is a relatively non expensive way of protecting your furniture.

To keep the rabbit away from the fridge or refrigerator, you can fix the cardboard in the opening. This will prevent the pet from entering the opening. Make sure you use a good quality cardboard.

This can prevent the pet from digging on the material of the furniture. You can also keep such barriers in front of various rooms. This will make sure that the pet can't enter these rooms. These are simple ways to keep the pet safe and also your things safe.

If you have recliners in your house, keep them away from the pet. The pet could be severely injured by these reclining chairs. The reclining action and the spring could injure the pet, especially the younger bunnies.

To be on the safer side, always check the chair or sofa that you are about to sit on. You don't want to sit on your bunny and injure him. Make sure he is not hiding under tables and sofas.

Keeping the Holland Lop away from house plants

You might be shocked to know that many varieties of plants are actually toxic to Holland Lop rabbits. Your rabbit doesn't know this and he might end up eating the most toxic plants.

Plants such as tulips and holly are extremely toxic for the Holland Lop rabbit. There are many other house plants that are poisonous for the Holland Lop. You should try to keep the bunny away from all kinds of house plants.

The best thing to do will obviously be to keep the plants in an area where the pet Holland Lop rabbit can't reach them. This is a fool proof way to keep them away from the plants.

If you find your beloved pet chewing on a house plant, you should stop him from doing so. It is a good idea to take him to the vet immediately to make sure that he is safe and sound.

Fences and walls

When your rabbit hutch is being positioned out in the open spaces of your house, there are a few precautions that you must take.

You should make sure that the hutch is not in proximity of the fences or walls. If the hutch is too close to the fence, some creature or animal might just get in.

Similarly, if the rabbit hutch is placed next to the wall, there will be no space for the air to circulate. This can be harmful for the pet in the long run.

You should remember that an outdoor enclosure will also be an invitation to many predators. You can't just keep the hutch outside and forget about it.

It is known that rabbits are often attacked by animals such as rats, snakes, weasels, voles, stoats, squirrels and mice amongst others.

These animals attack the bunny with the primary motive of stealing his food. These animals might also be looking for a shelter for themselves when the weather gets too nasty.

Another problem with housing these animals is that they bring along many mites, fleas and other disease causing bacteria and viruses. Weasels and stoats are capable of eating the poor bunny himself.

This makes it very important that the rabbit hutch is well protected. If you invest in a good quality hutch, this problem can be taken care of.

An initial investment will help you avoid many future problems. So, make sure that when you buy a hutch or get one made, you check the durability of the walls.

You can also keep the rabbit hutch in extra protection, especially during the night time. You can keep it in an area that is away from attack point of these predators.

You can make sure that the fences or walls that surround the rabbit hutch are strong enough. They should be sturdy enough to not allow any predator through them. The fences should be made of high quality mesh so that it is impossible to break them.

6. Bunny house rules

Rabbits are quick learners. They learn very fast as to what is expected from them and what is not. They also tune themselves accordingly.

It is important to understand here that you need to be patient with the bunny. As and when the bunny gets to spend more time with you, he learns more about you and the household.

The bunny will soon adapt to the routine you want to put him in. As the pet parent, you will also be aware that the rabbit can get naughty at times.

It is important to slowly introduce the pet to a schedule and a set of rules so that your family and the pet can live in harmony. This is an ideal situation for everybody.

You can teach your pet to stay out of certain rooms. Every time he does something that is not expected from him, you should repeat the word "no" several times. The Holland Lop will soon learn to associate no with things that can't be done.

He should know when he can expect his meals. For this to happen, you need to follow a fixed routine. You can't serve the rabbit his dinner one day at 7pm and the other day at 10pm. This will only confuse the poor pet.

No matter how much you read about keeping Holland Lop rabbits, your bunny will have a unique temperament. When you spend time with him, you will learn more about the animal. This will help you to tweak your attitude and also rules for him.

7. Extra stimulation through games and toys

If you notice your Holland Lop rabbit, you will see that he is very active during early mornings, late afternoons and some parts of the night.

These are the times when the Holland Lop rabbit wants to play with you or play with other rabbits. He wants to be social or look for food or just graze on his grass.

Exercise is critical for the Holland Lop rabbit. It should be noted that the rabbit should have access to enough space during these times in the day so that he can spend his energy in a constructive way.

A rabbit will stay happy and will keep you entertained as long as it has something to do. He should not be bored and his brain should be stimulated.

If the poor animal is confined to a corner and not allowed to do what it wishes to, he will suffer from boredom and then anxiety. This could further lead to serious depression in the rabbit.

Rabbits are like kids. They need different ways and items to keep them occupied and also entertained. They can also have a low threshold for tolerating things when bored.

You should find out ways to engage the Holland Lop rabbit in a way that he feel stimulated and excited.

You can try different games with him. You can also invest in some good quality toys for the Holland Lop bunnies to keep them occupied in a constructive way.

Benefits of toys for the Holland Lop rabbits

If you are still in two minds whether you want to get some toys for the bunny or not, then this section will help you to make an informed decision. You will be able to understand the benefits of toys for your Holland Lop rabbits, which are as follows:

- Domestic rabbits can suffer from something that can be termed as behavioural issues. You can significantly cure these issues if you are successful in actively engaging the brain of the bunny. Toys can help you to do that.

- You can also avoid your Holland Lop rabbit from acquiring behavioural issues by letting him play with toys that excite him and keep him mentally occupied.

- Along with keeping the mind healthy and also busy, the toys can play a significant role in keeping the body of the Holland Lop bunny healthy. The body will be engaged and hence will spend its energy in a positive way.

- You can also counterattack boredom by rotating games and toys. This way the bunny will have a different set of activities every other day. You should also spend some time understanding which toys your bunny likes the best. This will help you to know which toys to allow him at what times.

- There are different kinds of toys available in bunny pet shops. You can buy chewable toys that are made of good quality materials. These toys are safe for the pet. The Holland Lop bunnies will chew on them, thus helping them to wear down their teeth. This can also be an aid to their digestive system. The key is to invest in good quality and safe toys.

- You can also make toys for the pet. This can be a fun thing to do. This can be done easily with things that are found in your home.

Suitable toys for the bunny

This section will help you to understand the most suitable toys that you can allow your Holland Lop rabbits to play with.

The right kind of toys should be bought for the pets. You will get many ideas when you visit a shop that keeps toys for rabbits, but it is important that the toys are of good quality. They should not be harmful for the pet.

It is better if the toys are washable. This will enable you to wash the pet's toys every now and then when they are dirty. The harmful bacteria will also be removed from the toys when they are washed.

In addition, make sure that the toys can't be shredded by the animal. If the pet is able to shred the toy, he will swallow the shreds. This is very harmful and will only invite more trouble for the pet. To avoid all these issues, buy the right kind of toys.

You should remember that the furnishing should also be designed keeping in mind the comfort and also the security of the pet. The furnishing should not in any way disturb the lifestyle of the rabbit. It should gel with the personality of the animal.

A simple way to keep the rabbit happy is to give him an old t-shirt or piece of cloth. The pet will love it. He will act as if he is digging in the t-shirt. He will also try to fit in the t-shirt. This will keep him busy and happy.

Digging is a behaviour that is natural to a rabbit. They love to dig and mark their territories. This is done with chin and urine secretions and droppings. This helps them to have a sense of belonging.

You should provide things that can help the Holland Lop rabbit to cater to his digging needs. Get a sand box for him. You have no idea how happy your Holland Lop bunny will be.

When a rabbit digs in the sand, it naturally trims its nails. This is an added advantage of this recreational activity.

You should also invest in good quality tunnels, tubes and tents. This will also allow the rabbit to remain stimulated.

8. Hygiene and management

When you are hosting a pet, you also have to make arrangements to keep it and its surroundings hygienic. You should also be able to maintain the shelter of the pet well.

An unhealthy environment is a brooding ground for germs and disease causing viruses. It is better to keep the surroundings clean with some efforts rather than spending extra money on the pet's health treatment later.

This section will help you to understand how you can keep the rabbit hutch or rabbit house neat and clean.

First and foremost, the rabbit house should be such that it allows the rabbit to sleep in a separate place and defecate in a separate one.

The toilet in the rabbit house needs to be cleaned every single day. There should be no compromise in this regard. Such places, if kept unkempt, can lead to serious infections.

There are certain tasks that you need to do daily, while several others need to be done once a week. Similarly, if the food and water containers look dirty, they should be cleaned and refilled. It is best that you clean out the feeding and water containers on a daily basis.

The food and water must be replaced to prevent the bunny from eating any rotten or spoiled food. It is important that the cage is free from all bacteria and viruses that are known to cause diseases in pet animals. You should keep some time designated for the cleaning of the cage.

At least once a week, the litter and the bedding material should be changed. In case you notice any dampness in the bedding, it needs to be changed immediately. Damp areas encourage the growth of fungi. They are the primary cause for respiratory issues and skin troubles in bunnies.

To clean the shelter thoroughly, you have to start by dusting and dry cleaning. You will have to sweep the floor of the coop and dust off the ceiling.

All the fixtures, nest boxes, air inlets and fans must be dusted. The feed from the feeders should be removed. Any feces and debris is scraped off the floor and the perches. You can even vacuum the floor as an option.

Any area that is heavily soiled can be soaked with a low-pressure sprayer. Until the manure and dirt is softened, keep it soaked so you can remove it easily.

All the surfaces in the shelter should be cleaned out fully. Focus on the ceiling trusses, the windowsills and any area where dust may accumulate. Use a mild detergent with pH that ranges between 6 and 8. A mild alkali solution like a baking soda solution can be sprayed around to disinfect the shelter thoroughly.

Rinsing the soap off completely before you allow it to dry is a good idea. Use plain water to rinse and make sure that there aren't any puddles left behind in the shelter.

The shelter can be allowed to dry by air-drying the building. All the windows and vents should be opened. It is a good idea to use a fan or a blower if possible. The best option is to clean when the weather is warm and sunny. This improves the drying process.

Any repairs in the area should be made before you disinfect the shelter one final time. The rodent holes should be sealed, lighting fixtures must be repaired and any breakages or protruding areas in the construction must be repaired.

The most crucial step is the final disinfecting, which is usually overlooked by those who have a small hutch or cage. Once the whole shelter has been washed, rinsed and dried, you should use a good disinfectant.

Your veterinarian will be able to provide you with spray or fumigation options. The best option with most small shelters is to use a mild spray to disinfect it.

Make sure you follow the instructions provided by the manufacturer with respect to diluting the disinfectant. Usually you will need about one gallon of the diluted disinfectant per 200 square feet of space of the shelter.

Another point that you need to understand is that you should not use very strong disinfectants. Such products can be very harmful if they are ingested even in the smallest of quantities.

You should always look for mild anti bacterial soaps and detergents to clean the vessels and the floor.

If you want the process to be more thorough, you can even soak all the feeders and the bowls in 200-ppm chlorine solution. You can make that by mixing 1 tablespoon of chlorine bleach in a gallon of boiling water. With these steps, you should be able to raise a pet that is in the best of its health.

Chapter 5: Meeting the nutritional requirements of the Holland Lop rabbit

The diet of an animal is one of the key aspects of maintaining and improving his health conditions. If you don't feed your Holland Lop bunny good quality food in the right quantity, you would not be able to enjoy a healthy Holland Lop bunny around you.

The quality of life that the bunny will lead will depend on the food it is fed. It is as simple as that. You should focus well on the diet of the bunny to keep him healthy and happy. If you don't do so, you will see him deteriorating in all aspects of his life.

1. Busting common myths

When it comes to taking care of a bunny at home, there are many myths that you would have heard somewhere.

It is important to gain adequate knowledge so that you don't fall prey to any myths that circulate easily. Follow only what you are sure of and what your veterinarian recommends. You should not be playing with the health of the pet animal.

When it comes to diet of Holland Lop, there is a common myth. People tend to believe that rabbits only need carrots. They believe that carrot is the staple diet of a bunny. It is all he needs to stay healthy.

This is not right. Carrots are not the staple food. If you think that a rabbit fed on carrots will stay healthy, you are mistaken. Carrots should only be given to the pet as a treat.

2. Food requirements of the bunny

This section will help you understand the food requirements of your pet bunny in detail. This will help you to plan the meals of the pet in a better way.

Understanding the food pyramid

To make sure that you serve the right foods in the right quantities, it is very important that you understand the food pyramid of the animal.

Below the food pyramid lies the hay or grass. Eighty per cent of the diet of the pet bunny should constitute of timothy hay, meadow grass and alfalfa. The timothy hay and meadow grass should be provided in very good quantities.

In the food pyramid, above the grass or hay, you'll find herbs and green plants. Twelve per cent of the diet of the pet bunny should constitute of these two food items. This will allow you to limit high quantity of sugar and calcium in the diet.

Above the herbs and green plants, you'll find pellets. Six per cent of the diet of the pet bunny should constitute of pellets. You should give the pet a serving of one forth cup for every five pound of its bod weight.

Above the pellets, you'll find treats in the food pyramid. The remaining two per cent of the diet of the pet bunny should constitute of these treats. You can give the pet treats two times per week.

3. Importance of hay

Hay or grass is the main constitute of a Holland Lop rabbit's diet. You can't keep the rabbit healthy without the same.

Hay should be available to the pet bunny at all times. You don't have to keep a tab on how much hay the bunny eats.

The bunny will stop eating the hay or grass when it is full. But, it is important that it is available to him in unlimited quantities at all times.

Because hay is so important for the growth and development of the Holland Lops rabbit, it is only imperative that you understand why is it so important.

- Digestion: Each animal has a peculiar digestive system. This decides which foods the animal can digest and which foods it can't digest. The digestive system of the bunny is suited to break down fibre. Hay has a lot of fibre. So, eating the hay in large quantities gives the animal enough fibre that can be broken down by the digestive system.

- Dental health: Hay is very important for the dental health of a rabbit. When the animal chews on the hay, it wears down the bunny's teeth. This process is important to prevent dental disorders such as molar spurs.

4. Daily nutritional needs of the Holland Lop rabbit

The Holland Lop rabbit needs a diet that is rich in protein and fiber. The rabbits need the high amounts of protein to supplement the growth of fur. You can see a decrease in the quantity and quality of fur in the Holland Lop rabbit that is not fed high amounts of protein and fiber.

Fiber is also good for the general digestion of the animal. Sometimes, the rabbit can swallow some hair by mistake. The fiber in the diet of the pet will help him to avoid any harmful consequences because of swallowing of the hair.

The food habits of captive bunnies vary slightly from wild bunnies. As the owner of the pet, you have to make sure that the pet gets to eat what he ate in his natural habitat. Along with that, other foods should also be introduced to him.

Hay

Hay should be the main component of the Holland Lops rabbit's diet. It is important that he is allowed to eat as much hay as he wants to, as hay has many benefits for the rabbit. It is not possible to give the rabbit optimal nutrition by avoiding hay.

If the rabbit is eating good quantities of hay, he can save himself from intestinal blockages. Intestinal blockages can be very dangerous for the health of the rabbit. The issue of hairballs can also be controlled if the rabbit is eating good quantities of hay.

You should avoid Lucerne hay for the rabbit. It can cause diarrhoea in the rabbit if it is served in huge quantities.

Pellets

Pellets should also be served to the Holland Lop rabbit in the right quantities. You can serve half a cup to the rabbit every day.

If you are one of those people who buy pellets in bulk, then you should know the right way to store them. You should make sure that the pellets are safely stored in an airtight container because moisture can spoil the pellets.

If the pellets catch moisture, they will get mouldy. These kinds of pellets are not good for the Holland Lop because they can lead to diseases.

You will find guinea pig and rabbit mix in most stores. This is a mix of dried fruits, seeds, nuts and corn. Do not serve this to the Holland Lop. This kind of a mix is not required by the bunny. It can make the Holland Lop gain weight because of the high fat in the mix.

Pellets can be given to both the young and the adult rabbits. But, if you are not keen on serving the rabbits with the pellets, then make sure that at least the young rabbit is served these pellets. You can discontinue the use after the bunny matures.

A young rabbit should not be deprived of any nutrient as this is the growing stage, and you need to be cautious.

It should be noted here that if you wish to discontinue the use of pellets for the adult bunny, then you have to make sure that the Holland Lop rabbit is getting all the nutrition from the food it is eating. You should serve him good quality hay, vegetables and fruits to ensure that he is eating the right kinds of foods.

Fresh vegetables and fruits

It is advised to serve vegetables after the rabbit is three to four months of age. A Holland Lop rabbit loves to eat sweets. The fruits that you should serve him will do for the sweet requirement of the bunny.

You can serve the bunny a piece of apple, a few grapes or sultana at a time. You should make sure that you don't overdo it. If you serve large quantities of fruits to the rabbit, he might not be able to digest the same.

Vegetables are also essential for the bunny rabbit. You should make sure that you serve only high quality vegetables to the Holland Lop rabbit. Don't give him stale or spoilt vegetables because this will have a negative effect on his health.

You should look at serving him only organic vegetables and fruits. You can also grow your own vegetables if you have the space and time. The rule should be that if the vegetable or fruit is not fit for your consumption, it is not fit for the bunny's consumption.

5. Importance of Water

A Holland Lop rabbit needs good amounts of water for its survival. You should make sure that the animal always has access to drinking water.

Water helps the Holland Lop rabbit regulate its body temperature. The rabbit has a coat of fur over his body, and it is very important that the body of the pet maintains the right temperature.

If the Holland Lop rabbit is not hydrated well, he can develop severe health complications. You can even lose your pet Holland Lop rabbit because of a lack of water in his system. To avoid such things, make sure that the pet is hydrated at all times.

If you keep a water container in the hutch or cage of the pet Holland Lop rabbit, there is a high probability that the pet will play in the water. Even if he does not play, the water can spill easily in the cage or over the Holland Lop rabbit.

The water can wet the coat of the Holland Lop rabbit and it is important that the fur of the rabbit is always dry. The wet fur is the source of many health issues, especially skin-related diseases in the pet animal.

You should buy chew-proof water bottles for the Holland Lop rabbits. These bottles can be easily placed in the hutch or cage of the rabbit and are easily available.

It is easy to clean these water bottles. There are special brushes available in pet stores and also online that will allow you to clean the water bottles easily and without a fuss. Make sure that you clean them at least once a week.

You should also make sure that you purchase the right extensions to attach to the water bottle. These extensions will allow you to keep the water bottles in place and will also allow you to fix them at the right angle in the cage of the pet bunny.

If you live in a place where water freezes during winters, you will have to take special care of the Holland Lop rabbit. You might be busy in your work and all the water in the water bottle could be frozen.

Such a condition can force the pet to go without water for extended periods, which is extremely dangerous for the Holland Lop rabbit. A simple solution to this problem is to use heated bowls in winter, but with this the same issue of the coat getting wet arises. To make things simpler, you need to check at regular intervals that the water is not frozen.

Heatstroke

Water is considered an indispensable part of the bunny's meal plan. It has been noticed that they need more water than most other comparable species of animals.

To give you an idea of how important water is for your cute bunny, you should read the following fact. A five pound rabbit is known to drink as much water in a day as a twenty five pound dog can possibly drink.

The Holland Lop can easily consume fifty to one fifty millilitres of water in a day per two pounds of its body weight.

A rabbit is not able to sweat the way a human being can. This makes it more vulnerable to hot weather.

A rabbit is always better in cooler temperatures. Temperatures above 84 degree F can harm the pet in a very serious way.

This makes water all the more important for the bunny. The water consumption helps the bunny to keep its body temperature under control.

If you live in a country that experiences hot climates sometime during the year, you should make sure that you take care of the rabbit well, else he can suffer from a heat stroke.

Make sure that the rabbit has access to water 24 hours. He should never go without drinking water for more than a few hours.

6. Foods to avoid

You should make it a rule never to feed anything to the Holland Lop rabbit, unless you are sure that it is good for the rabbit. In many cases, people feed them certain foods assuming that if humans can consume them, then rabbits can.

However, this is not true. There are many food types that are good for humans and many other animals but not suitable for your Holland Lop rabbit. You will jeopardize the health of the pet if you are not careful about what you serve to him.

Sometimes, the children of the house can force the pet animal to consume toxic and unhealthy food items just for fun. This can prove to be fatal for the rabbit.

It is important that you keep a check on what the kids are doing with the pet animal. It is always advised to let the children interact with the rabbit under an adult's supervision.

Keep the food of the rabbit fresh, simple and healthy. When you are giving fruit, you should make sure that it does not have seeds because the seeds can be poisonous for the pet rabbit.

If you are looking for a comprehensive list of food items that are unhealthy for the rabbit, then the given list will help you. You should avoid these food items:

- Caffeine
- Bread
- Citrus peels
- Corn
- Fresh peas
- Grains
- Green beans and legumes
- Rice
- Nuts
- Rhubarb leaves
- Seeds

- Sugar
- Beets
- Chocolates and cocoa beans
- Onion and potatoes
- Avocado
- Cookies, cakes and candy.

You can also contact the 'Pet poison control' authority in severe cases.

7. Treats

Treats are an essential part of a pet's meal plan. Treats are like small meal gifts that make the pet happy and delighted. The anticipation of getting a treat can also keep his behavior in check.

You should work on giving your pet high quality treats. The treat should be tasty but also nutritious. The Holland Lop rabbit should look forward to receiving a treat from you. This section will give you an idea of the kind of treats you can include in your rabbit's meal plan.

It should be noted that just because your Holland Lop rabbit seems to enjoy a treat, you can't give the food item to him all day long. You will have to keep a check on the amount of treats a pet will get. This is important because treats are not food replacements, they are only small rewards.

It is also important that the pet associates the treat with a reward. He should know that he is being served the treat reward for a reason. You should also make sure that the treats are healthy for the pet.

If you keep serving him the wrong kinds of treats, it will only affect his health in the long run. This is the last thing that you would want as a parent of the pet.

The treat should have the right mix of vitamins, fatty acids, minerals and proteins. This will make the treat healthy and wholesome. It is better if the treat has no sugar content. This is because the sugar will add no food value to the treat. Such healthy treats can be given to the pet on a daily basis without any issues.

Be careful if you are planning to give your pet a bowl of nuts or fruits as a treat. If you think that all fruits can serve as a treat for the pet, then you are absolutely wrong. Though a small amount of certain fruits should be fine, a larger quantity will affect the health of the pet. You should avoid nuts because they are toxic for the Holland Lop rabbit.

The pet can suffer from diarrhea and other gastro intestinal problems because of consuming large amounts of toxic food. You will be shocked to know the problems that an undigested vegetable or fruit can cause in a Holland Lop rabbit.

If there is a piece of undigested food in the digestive tract of the animal, it can lead to obstructions and blockages. This will lead to many other digestive tract-related complications.

The bowel movements of the pet can be restricted or completely stopped because of the undigested food. This can even pose a very serious threat to the life of the animal.

You should also make sure that you peel and mash the items before you serve them to the animal. This will allow him to digest the food well. There have been many reports of blockages in rabbits because of undigested peels and seeds.

Chapter 6: Maintaining health of the Holland Lop rabbit

It is very important that you invest your time and energy in understanding the health requirements of the rabbit. This will allow your pet rabbit to enjoy a happier and healthier life.

There are a few diseases to which a Holland Lop rabbit is susceptible. An understanding of the symptoms and precautions of these diseases will help you to avoid them.

It should be understood that sometimes a rabbit can suffer for a very long time from a particular disease. This will make it very difficult to treat him later. No symptom should be ignored. You should take the pet animal to a veterinarian even at the slightest doubt.

This chapter will help you to understand how you can keep your pet healthy. You will be able to understand the symptoms, precautions and cure of common diseases that can affect your pet animal.

Being sensitive towards your pet's needs is one of the foremost responsibilities of a care giver. A rabbit will feel pain and trauma in very much the same way as you and me and as other mammals.

It is but critical that you prioritise your Holland Lop's health. If you see the pet in pain or if you feel that something is wrong with the pet, it is important that you act without any kind of delay.

Any pet care giver will be concerned about the overall welfare of the pet animal. Taking care of the health of the pet is an important and indispensable part of pet keeping. A healthy pet will be a happy pet. He will show improvements in various other departments.

This chapter will help you to understand the various health issues that a Holland Lop bunny can face. You will understand the various diseases and injuries that can inflict the pet bunny.

You should always remember that prevention is better than cure. A vet should always be in the loop when we are looking for ways to keep the pet bunny healthy. A vet's advice regarding all matters concerning the Holland Lop should be taken seriously.

1. Health check lists

One simple way of ensuring that the Holland Lop rabbit is in the best of its health is to check on him on a regular basis. This will ensure that you are able to detect even the slightest change in the pet's health. You should have a health check list that will help you to keep things in order.

The various checks or tasks that need to be done can be divided into three categories, daily/ weekly checks, monthly checks and annual checks.

In this section, we will go through all the checks that need to be done to ensure the pet is healthy and fine.

Daily/ weekly checks

Taking care of the health of the pet is an important and indispensable part of pet keeping. One simple way of ensuring that the rabbit is in the best of its health is to check on him on a daily or weekly basis.

Daily/ weekly checks category includes checks that need to be done daily or on a weekly basis. The idea of these checks is to make sure that you catch the slightest deviation of the pet animal from his normal state.

This section will help you to understand the various tests that you should be conducting. This can be done by you or another family member at your home.

The following checks should be done daily or at least once or twice a week:

- As a rule, check the eyes of the pet bunny. The underneath of the eye should have a pink colour. There should be no discharged from the eyes. Check for swelling, redness or discolouration.

- It should be noted that if the eyes of the pet are clouded, this could mean that the teeth of the Holland Lop have problems. Check the teeth of the bunny. They should not be crooked, loose, broken, overgrown or discoloured. A vet should be consulted in such cases.

- Check the nose of the bunny. The nose should be dry and clean. Check for discolourations and discharges.

- If the pet is sneezing frequently, then this could be an indication of an infection. In severe cases, it could indicate Sinusitis or Rhinitis. Blood tests done by the vet can confirm or deny the same.

- You should also check the rear end of the pet bunny on a regular basis. It should be clean and there should not be any sticking faeces or dirt. A bunny is known to self-groom, but if the pet gains a lot of weight, it is unable to do so. If you find faeces sticking to the pet on a regular basis, you should reduce the amount of caecotrophs in the pet's daily diet. During the summer months, you will have to perform this task two times in a day. This is because sticking faeces or dirt will attract flies. They will lay eggs on the sticky areas. These eggs will hatch into maggots in a few hours because of the heat. This, flystike, is known to be extremely dangerous for the bunnies.

- Keep a check on the faeces of the pet Holland Lop bunny. Early signs of an illness can be noticed by change in the colour or quality of faeces.

Monthly checks

While you are doing the daily and weekly checks, it is also important to do the monthly check-ups. This can be done by you or another family member at your home.

This section will help you to understand the various tests that you should be conducting and what you should be looking at to ensure that the pet bunny is healthy and happy.

- Check the fur or the skin of the bunny. There should be no lumps, fleas or flakes. The coat of the animal needs to be properly groomed and also very clean.

- Check the ears of the bunny. There should not be any flakes or build-up of wax. If there is any, you should consult the doctor.

- The nails of the pet should be short. Longer nails tear off and bleed easily. This leads to many complications and infections.

- The toes should also be correct. There should not be any abrasions or sores.

- Check the teeth of the bunny. They should be growing straight. They should not be crooked, loose, broken, overgrown or discoloured. There should not be any drooling, and the gums should be pink.

- The scent glands should also be examined. If there are dirty, you should clean them with cotton that is gently dipped in good quality mineral oil.

- The feet and legs of the bunny need to be carefully examined. It should be made sure that the pet is not limping. Check for abnormal stances and balance. Check the bottom of all the feet to make sure that there are no bare patches and that they are still covered with sufficient amounts of fur. The skin should not be red, which can indicate an infection.

- The underneath of the eye should have a pink colour. There should be no discharged from the eyes. Check for swellings, redness or discolouration.

- Check the nose of the bunny. The nose should be dry and clean. Check for discolorations and discharges.

- Check the heart beat with a stethoscope. The heart beat should be regular. You should learn what a normal heart beat for a rabbit is.

- Check the respiration of the animal. The breathing should be regular and clean. You should also learn what a normal respiration rate for a rabbit is.

- Check the body temperature of the Holland Lop rabbit. It should be normal.

- You should check the pet droppings. The normal droppings are large and moist. Small, dry and malformed droppings should be taken seriously.

- You should keep a check on the pet's urine. If you notice that the pet is having problems passing the urine, it can be a matter of concern.

The colour of the urine should be regular. It should be noted that the colour of urine of the pet varies. You need to know all the normal variations. For example, a red coloured urine is fine but red flakes and spots is not.

- You should also keep a check on the regular behaviour of the pet. Any change from the regular should be noted. Any change in movements or appetite should not be discarded. It is important to take advice from the veterinarian in such cases.

Annual checks

While you are religiously doing the daily and monthly checks, it is also important to do the annual check-ups. This should be done by a qualified vet.

You can speak to other rabbit owners to know about various local vets. You can read their testimonials online. This will give you an idea as to how well the vet can treat the rabbit.

Contact the local veterinarian centre and schedule an annual check up for the pet bunny with a qualified veterinarian. You should also have an idea of the procedure of the annual check so that you know what is happening with your beloved bunny.

You should provide the vet with written records of diet and previous medical issues of the Holland Lop. The vet will need to study the recent history of the pet. At this stage, you should also put forth your queries regarding your bunny.

If there are any doubts in your mind regarding the pet's recent behaviour and its effect on his health, you should not forget to share this with the doctor.

If your bunny is above the age of five years, the vet might suggest that complete body tests are done twice a year rather than just once a year.

The cost that you will encounter for the vet checkups and lab tests will be determined by various factors, such as your location and the health condition of your pet. It is always advised that you insure your rabbit to take care of unforeseen circumstances.

Physical examination

After the overview of recent history of the pet's health conditions, the vet will proceed to conduct the physical examination of the lop rabbit.

The teeth are examined for the very common malocclusion and the lips for signs of swelling, drooling, abrasions and sores.

It is believed that the eyes of the pet are an index to his health. The vet should examine the eyes closely for any visible or subtle symptoms of an impending disease.

The eyes should be closely examined for any discharge or tearing. Infections and swelling of conjunctiva and obstructions of tear ducts should not be ignored.

The skin and fur should be thoroughly examined. The vet would check for any visible signs of parasites and termites.

He would also test whether the pet has been biting or scratching itself. Hair loss, fur shedding and lesions are also examined. You should make sure that the vet examines under the tail and back of the neck also.

It should be noted here that the vet also should know the sex of the rabbit. It should not be assumed. The tail should be lifted and checked for this.

The legs and toes of the rabbit are palpated in case there are any abnormal lumps. The vet should also listen to the lungs and heart with the help of a stethoscope. Palpation of the abdomen should be done to evaluate the shape and size of the organs.

Lab tests

If the veterinarian diagnoses any abnormalities, it is advised that laboratory tests are conducted. Blood tests, urine tests and testing of bacteria cultures might have to be conducted. This will help you to eliminate or ascertain a health issue in the Holland Lop bunny.

The vet will also test stool samples of the rabbit as a routine. If a rabbit is always kept indoors this might not be necessary at every visit.

2. Identifying and treating injuries in the Holland Lop rabbits

An unhealthy pet can be a nightmare for any owner. As the prospective owner or the owner of a beautiful Holland Lop rabbit, you might be thinking about what you can do to ensure that the pet is always in the prime of its health. You can contribute a great deal to the health of the animal.

The food that you provide the animal with, the conditions that you keep him in and the love that you give him will all affect the general well being and the health of the Holland Lop rabbit.

You should always make sure that your pet is always kept in a clean environment. A neat and clean environment will help you to keep off many common ailments and diseases. Also, make sure that the pet is well fed at all times.

When you are looking to maintain the health of your pet Holland Lop rabbit, then you should make an attempt to understand the common health issues that the animal faces. This will help you to prepare yourself well and also treat your pet well.

It is important that you take care of your pet's health. The pet will depend on you for most of its needs. It will not be able to tell you if it is facing any discomfort regarding its health. You should be able to identify the symptoms of various diseases in your pet to treat it well.

You should also be able to diagnose any symptoms of injuries in your pet. If you can treat him in your home, then you should do it very carefully. In case you have any doubts, you should take the pet to the veterinarian.

As you would have understood by now that your Holland Lop rabbit is a very mischievous animal. He will lead a very active lifestyle. The pet likes hopping and jumping around. He will also enjoy exploring things around him.

All the traits of the bunny make it susceptible to many injuries. There is nothing to worry if your pet animal injures itself. You should be able to diagnose the injuries so that they can be treated well.

Never commit the mistake of ignoring an injury or a symptom. Even if you have the slightest doubt, you should always act on it. It is always a good idea to take the Holland Lop rabbit to the veterinarian if you spot something unnatural with the pet.

It is important that you learn the basics of diagnosing the injuries. This is important because if a small injury is treated well, the Holland Lop rabbit can be saved from a major problem in the future.

You should be on the lookout for any symptoms that your Holland Lop rabbit might display when it is injured. These symptoms could mean that there is something wrong with your bunny.

It is important that you understand that your pet animal might not show any signs of injuries, even when it is injured. It will be your responsibility to diagnose the injury before it turns into a bigger problem.

Understand some basic signs of injuries, stress and diseases in the pet Holland Lop rabbit. This will help you to get the pet treated on time. If the pet is treated on time, you can avoid many future problems.

Is your pet looking very lazy and lethargic? Is your Holland Lop rabbit looking very disturbed? This could be because he has injured himself and is in pain.

The pet might injure himself with a chair or other furniture while playing. The limbs of the animal could also be hanging. This is also a clear sign of injury to the pet. You should closely examine his limbs to be sure.

Is your pet stumbling? Is the pet showing uncoordinated movements? If you find these symptoms, then you know that the pet has some issue. Take him on your lap and gently check his limbs.

If there is a change in the way he sits or stands or carries himself, then this could also mean that the injury has forced the pet to change the way he usually is. This could be because he is in pain.

You should look out for the faeces of the animal. If there is any change in the colour of the faeces, this could mean that there is something wrong with the health of the pet.

Do you witness any changes in the skin of the pet? If yes, then this could also mean that there is something that needs your attention. Don't overlook anything that does not seem very natural.

Do you spot any blood on the skin of the animal? Does the fur of the pet look different? You should look for blood stains in the enclosure of the animal also. This could mean that something is not right. Look for certain common symptoms, such as coughing and vomiting by the animal.

If you pet looks scared and tensed, you should understand that it is for a reason. You need to closely examine him to find out what is wrong.

When you spot any of the given symptoms in your pet, you should know that something is not right. You will have to take a closer look at the pet and examine. This examination will help you to understand if there is something wrong with your pet.

While you are examining your pet, you should also understand that your pet could be scared. It is important that you make the pet feel comfortable. This will help you conduct the examination properly and without any problems.

To make sure that the pet animal is not terrified when you are trying to examine him for any potential injuries, you should make sure that you conduct the examination in a closed area, a place where the animal feels safe and protected. You should try to examine him indoors.

Make sure that all the tools that are needed for the examination are ready. You shouldn't leave your pet alone to fetch the tools. Everything should be ready before the examination.

The noise level around you should be as low as possible. The noise will stress the pet and will irritate him, so make sure there is no noise around. Conduct the examination in a quiet place. This is important to keep things under control.

Do not let the place be crowded when the examination is being conducted. Make sure that all the other pets and your family members are outside and not in the same place where the examination is being conducted.

If the animal sees you being fidgety, it will only add to his stress. Be as gentle and kind as possible. This will help your pet to relax and feel less stressed. You should in no way add to the stress and pain of the pet.

You should be as calm and as confident as possible. Your confidence will give him some hope and relief. These are some very simple tips, but will go a long way in ensuring that the pet is being handled well.

You should check his entire body. Remember to check on both sides of the body. Start the examination at one particular point and then move ahead from that point. The examination should be definite and guided and not random.

Look at how your pet responds to the body examination being done. If you feel that the animal is not taking it too well, you should stop the examination. You should look for any stress signs that he displays.

It is important that you don't ignore any symptoms. It is also important that you don't force anything on the pet; otherwise the animal can go into deep shock. After your initial check-up, if you find something wrong then visit the veterinarian.

You should never self-treat the pet. This could complicate things further. Take the pet to the veterinarian because he is the best judge of the pet's condition. Discuss your doubts and confusions with the vet.

Veterinary care

If you wish to keep your Holland Lop rabbit happy and healthy, you need specialized veterinary care to do so. While a regular vet will be able to provide you with temporary relief during an emergency, you will need a qualified veterinarian that practices medicine on rabbits.

You need to find a veterinarian that understands your concern for your pet rabbit. So, when you are in talks with a vet who can potentially become the one to take care of your rabbit, remember to discuss your doubts with him/her.

Don't wait for the pet to fall sick. It is always a good idea to choose a veterinarian for the animal in advance. If your pet falls sick or encounters an injury, you should know where to take him. The last thing you want to do is to search for a vet when the pet's condition is deteriorating.

The best way to find a good veterinarian is to go by the breeder's suggestion. A good breeder will always consult a good vet, and will suggest the same to you.

It is important that the veterinarian has good experience of working with bunnies. Many of them might have the knowledge, but might lack in practical experience. It is your duty to make sure that the vet holds a good name amongst other owners of rabbits.

While you are choosing your veterinarian, you should also consider the distance of the clinic to your home. You would want to consult a vet who is good and also close to your home.

3. Common diseases in Holland Lop rabbits

This section will help you to understand the various common health problems that your pet rabbit can suffer from. As the caregiver, you should attempt to understand these diseases in detail so that you can provide the animal with the right care.

Pasteurellosis

Holland Lop rabbits are prone to Pasteurellosis. It is one of the most common diseases known to affect rabbits across various species. It is also known as sniffles.

It can be controlled easily with the help of a few precautions and measures. Once the pet acquires this disease, it keeps spreading if the condition is not treated.

Cause

The cause of Pasteurellosis or sniffles is a bacterium that is known as Pasteurella multocida. This bacterium attacks the respiratory system of Holland Lop rabbits.

It is also known that there are different strains of this bacterium. These strains can have a deadly effect on various parts of the rabbit's body, such as ears and the eyes.

If this disease spreads to the eyes of the Holland Lop rabbit, he can acquire Conjunctivitis. On the other hand, if this disease spreads to the ears of the Holland Lop rabbit, he can experience head tilting and severe disorientation.

Symptoms

It should be noted that the symptoms of the disease will depend on the strain of bacteria that affect the rabbit. You can look out for the following general symptoms in the rabbit to know if he is suffering from this particular disease:

- The animal will have a runny nose. This is one of the first symptoms of the disease.
- The animal will sneeze a lot.
- If you go near the animal, you will hear him snoring or sniffling while he breathes.
- The rabbit can experience sores or abscesses on his respiratory tract. This will also be very painful.
- He can experience head tilting and severe disorientation.

Treatment

This particular disease can be controlled easily with the help of antibiotics. You should consult a veterinarian as soon as you catch the symptoms of the disease. It should be noted that ignored symptoms can lead to a severe case of Pasteurellosis.

The veterinarian will keep the pet rabbit on a supplementary biotic and antibiotic course for the duration of four to about thirty days. This will depend on the severity of the disease.

Calcivirus

Calcivirus is also known as VHD or viral haemorrhagic disease. Calcivirus is more prevalent in wild rabbits. It is a viral disease, which can turn extremely lethal if not treated on time.

Cause

The disease is caused by a virus, as the name itself suggests. It can affect the lymph nodes in a very drastic way. In severe cases, the liver can be completely damaged.

If the disease is allowed to spread, it will affect the blood of the animal. The blood will not coagulate. This in turn will affect many other organs of the pet animal.

Symptoms

The following symptoms will help you to confirm whether your pet is suffering from this health condition:

- The virus can lead to inflammation of the intestine, which gets worse with time if it is not treated.
- The pet will also experience a high fever.
- As the disease progresses, the pet will lose his energy and will appear more and more lethargic.

Treatment

If you notice any of the given symptoms in your pet rabbit, you should take him to the veterinarian. He/she will take a blood sample of the animal and test it for the disease, along with other tests.

Though the disease can be controlled to some extent, there is no specific treatment for this particular disease. It is suggested to sanitize the habitat of the pet thoroughly, as maintaining hygiene will help to keep this disease-causing virus away from the pet rabbit.

Scours

Scours is one of the most common diseases known to affect rabbits across various species. This condition is characterized by excessive diarrhea in the rabbits.

This is a bacterial disease and can be controlled easily with the help of few precautions. If you give your bunny a proper and healthy diet and also try to maintain optimal hygiene conditions around him, you can definitely avoid this health condition in the pet.

Cause

The main reasons behind scours are unhealthy diet and poor hygiene conditions. If the pet is suffering from a severe case of viral or bacterial infection, scours could be one of the side effects of the infection. In such cases, it is best to treat the infection if you want to treat this condition.

Another common cause of this health condition in bunnies is stress and overheating. When your pet is going through excessive stress, it will lead to scours.

If there is poor hygiene around the pet, it can also lead to scours. You should try to maintain optimum hygiene levels at all times. If the pet is suffering from some other infection or health condition, scours could be a side effect of the health condition.

Symptoms

The following symptoms will help you to confirm whether your pet is suffering from this health condition:

- One of the early symptoms of this disease includes diarrhea. If your pet is suffering from diarrhea that you are not able to control, then your pet could be suffering from scours.

- You should keep a check on the stools of the rabbit. The color and texture of the stools will help you determine whether the rabbit has scours or not.

-

Treatment

If your pet rabbit is suffering from excessive diarrhea or scours, you would have to take certain measures to solve this issue. He should be given electrolytes. The electrolytes will help to give the body the salts that it might have lost because of the condition.

It is advised to administer probiotics to the animal. This will help to treat his condition.

Once your pet starts getting better, you should make sure that it is given a very healthy diet. A good diet can prevent scours. You can even consult your veterinarian if your pet doesn't get well. The medication given by the doctor will help the pet to get better soon.

Make sure that all the necessary nutrients are given to the pet. You can also look to give him supplements if his diet does not provide the right nutrition.

Infestation with mites

Holland Lop rabbits are also prone to mites. Mites can lead to skin irritation in the beginning and then severe skin allergy if not treated.

It is not a very deadly disease and can be controlled easily with the help of a few precautions and measures. Once the pet acquires this disease, it keeps spreading if the condition is not treated.

Symptoms

You can look out for the following symptoms in the rabbit to know that he is suffering from this particular disease:

- Inflammation of the skin because of the infection caused by mites makes the pet irritable and restless.

- It is a skin disease, so a change in the texture of the skin on the pet could be an indication of an infection. In most cases, the skin starts getting red.

- You will notice dandruff patches on the skin of the rabbit. You should look at the nape of the neck and the base of the animal's tail, where the patches will be very prominent.

- As the condition worsens, the patch size will increase.
- The pet will scratch again and again at one spot. You will find the pet to be very irritated and agitated. The skin could also develop rashes or scales.

Treatment

The skin disease can be treated by the use of mild medicated soaps. These soaps will soothe the skin and will also treat the infection.

There are some creams that can also help to treat the skin and make the condition better. In severe cases, certain ointments might have to be applied to the skin. You should also take care of the diet of the pet.

A good diet will help the skin to heal itself faster. In case the skin gets worse with time then you will have to consult the veterinarian. He might suggest some oral medicines to heal the skin faster.

He might also suggest some special ointments that will give some relief to the pet. The use of 'Ivermectin' is recommended for the rabbits. It helps the skin to get rid of mites faster.

It is also suggested to clean the habitat of the pet after the pet is treated. This is to avoid any relapse of the skin disease.

You should also focus on grooming the animal. This also helps the animal to get rid of dead cells, thus lowering the chance of an infestation of mites.

Urine burn

Urine burn is also common in rabbits. When the urine of the rabbit soaks the fur, it leads to this particular condition.

This can further lead to inflammation of the skin, which gets worse with time if it is not treated. The pet will also experience severe hair loss.

Symptoms

You can look out for the following symptoms in the rabbit to know whether he is suffering from this particular disease:

- Inflammation of the skin because of the infection makes the pet irritable and restless.
- His private areas will appear sore and red. This is one of the most common symptoms of the disease.

Treatment

The burn can be treated by the use of mild medicated soaps. These soaps will soothe the skin and will also treat the infection.

There are some soothing creams and ointments that can help to treat the skin and make the condition better. You should also take care of the diet of the pet.

In case the skin gets worse with time then you will have to consult the veterinarian, who may suggest oral medicine.

It is also suggested to keep the habitat of the pet clean. This is to avoid any relapse of the skin disease. The cage needs to be dry and clean at all times.

Pneumonia

The rabbit is also highly susceptible to pneumonia, especially when the bunny is young. If your bunny shows symptoms of a respiratory disorder, you should look for various symptoms of this disease.

It can be caused by bacteria of a virus that thrives in dirty and unsanitary conditions. This is the reason why it is always advised to keep the hutches clean and sanitary.

The main cause of this health condition is damp hutches and cages. If the living conditions of the pet are not good, he can suffer from this disease.

It is important that you treat this disease because it is known to be a life-threating condition. If you discover any respiratory disorders in your pet, you should take the issue seriously because as the disease reaches its advanced stages, it becomes more difficult to treat.

Symptoms

You should be on the lookout for the following symptoms to confirm the presence of the disease in your rabbit:

- If your pet animal refuses to eat, then this could be because of this disease. The pet will suffer a drastic loss of appetite.

- Is your pet being very lazy and lethargic? Is he refusing to move? This could also be because of this disease.

- The pet will have difficulty breathing. There could be a blockage or congestion in the chest area. This is a very common symptom and should be taken very seriously.

- The pet could be suffering from a high temperature. This is also a very common symptom accompanying pneumonia.

- The pet might vomit the food that he is fed. This is because of the congestion in his chest.

Treatment

There is treatment available if your rabbit is suffering from pneumonia. The type of treatment that will be chosen will depend on a few factors. If the pneumonia is too severe, then a different treatment is chosen in comparison to if it is not too severe.

The vet will recommend antibiotics to combat the disease. The dose and strength of the antibiotic will depend on the severity of pneumonia in the pet bunny.

If the bunny is not able to recover and is already at an advanced stage, then the dose of antibiotic is injected directly through the skin. This is known to work rapidly on the animal.

Ringworm

Ringworms are a very common issue that can affect your pet rabbit. Ringworms can attach themselves to the rabbit. This will cause immense discomfort to the rabbit.

While many people don't consider this as a major health issue, ringworms should never be ignored. They are known to be very dangerous. They can be a potential threat to your other pets as well. You should make sure that ringworms are treated well and on time.

If you believe that ringworm is a worm, then you are wrong. It is a fungus and fungal treatment is required to get rid of ringworms. If you are treating your pet for worms, then you will not be able to combat this condition.

The problem with this disease is that it can get worse with time, so it is important that you treat it as soon as possible. If ringworms are allowed to grow on the animal, they will lead to a lot of fur loss.

Causes

There are many causes that could be behind the ringworms attacking your pet. One of the most common causes of ringworms is contact with animals already infested with the same.

Ringworms can easily travel from one carrier to another, so if an animal infested with ringworms comes into contact with your bunny, he can easily get them too.

Symptoms

You should be on the lookout for the following symptoms to confirm the presence of ringworms on your rabbit:

- Is your rabbit scratching itself too much? Does your pet seem as if he has an itch? Do you see some area red with itchiness and scratching?

- Do you find him irritable and uneasy? If the answer is yes, then your rabbit could be infected with ringworms.

- Ringworms make the animal itchy and too much itchiness can develop red sores on the body. You should be on the lookout for such obvious symptoms of ringworms.

- The pet will slowly develop bald patches. You should be on the lookout for this symptom. It is one of the most common symptoms of the rabbit being infected with ringworms.

- The head of the bunny is most likely to be affected. It will slowly spread to other parts of the body. You should look out for bald patches on the head.

Treatment

If you find the given symptoms on your pet then you can be convinced that your pet has been infested with ringworms. It is important that you take the steps to help your pet get rid of them. If you do not treat the pet soon, then they will only trouble the poor animal more. You can successfully treat the pet by following an antifungal treatment for the disease.

You should not allow the pet to come into contact with other pets of the house. The ringworms can spread very easily. Human beings can also easily catch them. You should wear gloves when you go near the pet.

If you find any of the above symptoms in a rabbit, it is important that you waste no time and take the pet to the veterinarian. The vet will conduct some tests to confirm the condition.

He/she will suggest an antifungal cream that will help to get rid of the ringworms. The hair or fur in the affected area needs to be tied so that the ringworms don't spread to other parts of the body.

Hair loss

Another common problem that your Holland Lop rabbit can go through is hair loss. Though this might not seem like a big problem, hair loss is generally an indication of other serious problems. Therefore, it is important that you don't take the issue lightly. You should make an attempt to understand the causes of hair loss so that you can work on eliminating those issues.

If your rabbit is very young, hair loss could be an indication that your pet has been kept in extremely warm temperatures. The young pet might not be taking the warm environment well.

If your Holland Lop rabbit is not too young, then hair loss could be an effect of some other health issue. You should understand these issues. The most common reasons behind hair loss are unhealthy diet and too much stress.

Causes

One of the most common causes of hair loss in Holland Lop rabbits is lack of a healthy diet. You have to make sure that your pet is fed properly so that it can be in its optimum health and glory.

Another common cause of hair loss in Holland Lop rabbit is stress. The first things that you should look into after you spot hair loss are the diet and the stress levels of your pet. Apart from these two common causes, there are a few other causes of hair loss in the animal. If your pet is facing some skin allergy or has skin irritation, it can lead to hair loss.

It is also known that fungal infections lead to drastic hair loss. If your pet has suffered from some fungal infection in the recent past, then this could be the cause of hair loss in the pet.

Sometimes, a large amount of bleach is present in soap items. This bleach is harmful for the Holland Lop rabbit. You should also check the amount of bleach that is present in the soap that is used to wash things that often come into direct contact with your pet. For example, you can check the amount of bleach present in the soap powder that is used to wash the water container and the food container of your Holland Lop rabbit.

Symptoms

The most obvious symptom of hair loss in an animal is the reduction of hair on the body. You might spot hair all over the place.

- If you spot a bald patch on your Holland Lop rabbit, then your pet has been suffering from hair loss.

- You should also look for hair loss in bigger and larger areas.

Treatment

If you spot hair loss in your Holland Lop rabbit, you should immediately look for the direct or indirect causes behind the same. There can be many causes of hair loss, thus the treatment accordingly varies. You should make a thorough check on the living conditions of the pet. This will help you to understand the problems that he is facing and the causes behind the hair loss. You might be required to make changes and adjustments on the basis your evaluation. If the cause of the hair loss is food related, then make sure that you work on providing the pet with a wholesome and nutritious diet.

If the cause behind the hair loss is a fungal infection, then you have to make sure that the infection is treated and eliminated. You should apply suitable anti-fungal topical creams for treating the fungal infection well.

If the Holland Lop rabbit is stressed, then the most obvious treatment to reduce and stop hair loss will be to reduce the stress of the Holland Lop rabbit. You would have to understand the reasons that could be behind the pet being so stressed. You will be required to make appropriate changes in the pet's living conditions to improve his health and reduce his stress levels.

Fleas or lice

As you might know, if an animal is infested with fleas or lice, it can get very difficult and uncomfortable for the animal. Fleas also lead to other issues and problems. Your Holland Lop rabbit can catch fleas or lice easily if it comes into contact with other domesticated animals. For example, if you have a pet dog or a pet cat along with the rabbit, then there is a strong chance that your rabbit caught the fleas from them.

Both fleas and lice are parasites that can irritate animals. It can be very easy for your pet to get these parasites, but the good news is that a common treatment can help you to get rid of both these parasites. Another important point that you need to understand is that even after you treat these parasites, the infection can re-occur. It is important to work on the cause of these annoying parasites.

Causes

One of the most common causes of infestation is the contact with animals already infested with the parasites.

Symptoms

The following symptoms will help you to confirm whether your pet is suffering from a parasite infestation:

- The skin of the pet will start to get red. Look for red spots on different areas of the pet. The red areas could also be swollen.

- Does your pet appear itchy? Is he irritated and annoyed? Is he itching more than usual? If the answer to all these questions is yes, then this could be a parasite infestation.

- Does the pet seem visibly irritated? The parasites will make the pet very irritable. He might seem like he is being very moody, but in actual fact it is the irritation caused by the fleas and the lice.

Treatment

If your rabbit is suffering from a parasite infestation by either fleas or lice, you don't need to worry, as it can be treated. You need to make sure that you work on the cause of the parasites also; otherwise the parasites can strike again.

If the other domestic animals in the house have passed on the infestation to the rabbit, then you should make sure that these pets are also treated for the parasite infestation. If you don't do so, there will be a second infestation.

Both fleas and lice can be treated with the same remedy. You would need to apply a special powder to the affected areas of the rabbit. The powder will cool down the area, repair the skin and will also help to disable the fleas and the lice so that they don't create any further damage.

The special powder that needs to be applied on the pet is pyrethrum or carbaryl powder. You can even consult your veterinarian if you think that the infestation is becoming serious.

Coccidiosis

One of the most common health problems in rabbits is the Coccidiosis. This particular health problem is caused by protozoa Cocci, which have only one single cell.

It is important to know that there are nine types of Cocci that can affect rabbits. Eight out of these nine types are known to affect the intestines of the bunnies. The ninth type of Cocci can affect the liver of the rabbit.

You should also know that cats, dogs and chickens can also be affected by Cocci. It is important to note that young rabbits are often more susceptible to Cocci.

Older bunnies have immunity against this disease, so if you have a young rabbit, then you should be worried about this health issue. It is important that you understand the causes and ways to avoid this disease.

Causes

One of the most common causes of this disease is an unclean enclosure. If the cage or the hutch of the rabbit is not cleaned for days, you can expect your rabbit to get infected with this disease.

The parasite will dwell in dirty areas. The rabbit will ingest the egg of the disease-causing parasite. They will do so when they lick or eat from dirty cage floors or when they eat contaminated hay.

While the adult rabbit is less likely to suffer from this condition, it can be a carrier. It can shed the eggs of the parasite in its feces. This can further infect other pet rabbits in the vicinity.

The eggs of this disease-causing parasite can thrive and survive for over a year in a humid and warm environment. This makes it all the more important that you regularly clean the surroundings of the rabbit.

Symptoms

You can look out for the following symptoms in the bunny to know whether he is suffering from this particular disease:

- The pet will lose his appetite. You will find him avoiding even his favorite foods. He will not drink water, which could further lead to dehydration.

- You will notice sudden and drastic weight loss in the pet. This is one of the most common symptoms of this condition.

- Another symptom of this disorder is vomiting. The pet will throw up from time to time.

- The pet would be seen struggling during his bowel movements. You should watch out for this symptom.

- You will notice the bunny being very lazy and lethargic.

- You can spot your rabbit sitting in one corner with a hunched back. His feet will be forward, and he will appear to be really sad and sick.

- The pet will suffer from diarrhea. You might also notice blood in the stools of the rabbit.

Treatment

If you find any of the above symptoms in a rabbit, it is important that you waste no time and take the pet to the veterinarian. The vet will conduct some tests to confirm the condition. The most common treatment of this condition includes the use of corid powder. You can get it easily at all pet store. Sulfamethoxide is also used to help the pet recover from this condition.

It should be mixed with water and given to the pet rabbit for seven days. After the first cycle, a break of over seven days is taken. After that, the mix needs to be given for another seven days.

Most veterinarians will suggest completing these two cycles at least once in six months. This ensures that the rabbit does not get this health condition again. This is all the more important in young bunnies.

If your female bunny is pregnant, you should not administer this particular drug to the doe. It can be given to her once she is in the lactating phase.

It is important that you don't ignore any symptom and consult the vet as soon as possible. Always try to maintain cleanliness in the hutch of the pet rabbit.

Chapter 7: Training the Holland Lop rabbit

No matter how much you read about an animal, your pet will have some individual characteristics that will separate him from the rest of the lot. The training phase can be a great opportunity for you to learn more about your pet.

It may take weeks or months before you see any positive results. If you fail to be kind towards him during the training process, he will detest coming to you and things will only get worse.

Don't punish the rabbit if he fails to follow you. You should remember to have fun even during the training phase. You shouldn't be too harsh on your pet.

The pet might slip into sadness and depression if severe training sessions continue. This will hamper the pet's emotional bond with you and also his health.

Rabbits generally associate chasing with being held captive. When you are training the rabbit, try not to chase him.

1. Litter training

As the owner, you are also the caretaker and the parent for the pet. You will have to teach him stuff that he needs to know when living in a family. Don't get upset when you see your rabbit littering all around. You can train him to not do so.

To begin with, you should buy a few litter boxes. Keep these boxes in various areas of the house where the rabbit is most likely to litter. You should cover the various corners where you have found the litter previously. In addition, install one box in the cage. Eventually, you want the rabbit to litter in the cage itself.

It is believed that a Holland Lop rabbit will generally litter in the first fifteen or twenty minutes of waking up. So, there is a chance that the rabbit has already littered in the box in the cage. When you open the cage to take him out, check the box and wait until he has used the box.

You should signal the animal by pointing towards the litter box. The pet should slowly realize that he needs to use the box if he wants to get out of the cage. You should wait near the cage until he is all done.

Another point that you need to understand here is that rabbits are very smart. When the rabbit understands that you will let him out of the cage once he uses the litter box, he might pretend to use it. You need to check the box and make sure that he has actually used it.

If you notice that the pet is not using the litter box installed in his cage, then you need to understand why. There is a chance that the litter box is uncomfortable for him. In such a case, you should look to buy a box with a front ledge that is low. This is good for your rabbit.

You can even make one. If you buy a cat litter box, you will notice that the front ledge is not too low. You could cut it in half to make it suitable for your rabbit. The idea is to make it really comfortable for your pet rabbit. A suitable litter box will have a back ledge that is high. This gives the right support to the pet.

The rabbit will take its own time to adjust to the environment. It is always difficult for a new pet to adjust. If you get him a new cage or if you make any changes in his surroundings, he will find it difficult to adjust, but this problem is only time related and will get solved.

Every time the rabbit litters outside the box, place his litter in the box that he should be using. You need to show the pet that he should be using the litter box. This could be difficult for you in the beginning, but the rabbit will learn quickly. You should place food and toys in areas and corners that you want to save.

When the rabbit sees a toy or a food item in a corner, he will try to look for another corner to pass his stool. You can also place a mat underneath the litter box to save your carpet or home mats. Make sure that the mat that you use is waterproof.

Observe your rabbit's mannerisms when he is using the litter box. If he has a tendency to bite the mat underneath or stuff kept around, you should discourage this behavior. To do so, you can use bitter food sprays on the mats and other stuff. This will automatically discourage the pet from biting around when he is littering.

The litter box of the rabbit should definitely be kept clean to maintain the overall hygiene and to prevent diseases. You should wash the box once a week. Yet, a point that needs to be noted here is that the box should not be too clean. A clean litter box that almost appears new could be appealing to you, but it is a turn off to the rabbit.

The rabbit will use its sense of smell to use the areas that he has used before. You should leave some paper litter in the box to encourage the pet to use the box again. This is a simple trick that you can use when you are trying to litter train your pet.

When you are buying a litter box, you should remember that the size of the box will depend on the size of your rabbit. For example, a male pet rabbit will need a bigger box due to his size compared to the box that a female pet rabbit will need.

If you are domesticating more than one rabbit in your home, then this will also affect the littering process of the rabbits. This may come as a surprise to you, but the dominant pet could affect how the other pets use the litter boxes in the house.

You might notice that the habits of a dominant pet rabbit are influencing the other pet rabbits. The dominant one will always try to boss around and make the others feel inferior.

Rabbits don't like to use the same litter box. The rabbits could also be competing for a litter box. These are the issues that you will have to find out. Observe which rabbit is using which litter box and which one suddenly leaves a litter box.

You should make sure that each rabbit has his own box, so that he not left to use the carpets and the floors. Even after you have trained your rabbit to use the litter box, you have to be vigilant.

If you are observant, you might face issues. There could be instances when your pet would suddenly give up the use of the litter box. Instead of getting angry with him, it is important that you probe into the reason for his sudden change in behavior.

When the pet is sick, he might give up the use of the litter box. The main reason behind this is that the pet might not have the strength in his hind legs to get on to the box. He could be suffering from a gastro intestinal or adrenal disease, which could make him weak and lethargic.

You should be cautious when you observe such changes in your pet rabbit. Don't ignore his condition, or don't force him to use the litter box. You should not get angry at the pet because he is littering on the floor. It is not his fault if he is not well.

The best thing to do in such a situation is to take the pet to the vet. This will prevent the condition getting worse. He/she will look for the symptoms of various diseases and will help you to understand what is wrong with the pet.

The given process will take some days, but you will have to have some patience. The idea is to help the pet get used to the food before you can expect the pet to eat the food. Once he is gets used to it, he will try out the food item on his own.

2. Training rabbit against biting

When you buy new Holland Lop rabbit, you might notice that the animal has a tendency to bite things. This is a very natural behaviour of a rabbit. They try to bite and chew everything. So, you shouldn't be very surprised.

You will see him trying to chew everything he can, such as furniture and plants. He will not even hesitate to chew wires, which can be very harmful for him. This is the reason why the rabbit needs to be supervised.

As explained earlier, a Holland Lop rabbit can exhibit such behaviour when they are scared. It should be noted that if the Holland Lop rabbit has had a history of abuse then you can expect him to chew and bite more in fear than in a playful mood.

If the Holland Lop rabbit bites you real hard you can have a real bad wound. This makes it all the more important to train the pet. There are many Holland Lop rabbits that are beaten up and abused. If you have rescued one such animal, then you will definitely find him trying to bite you out of fear and tension.

But, don't worry because this is a passing phase. The love and warmth he will get at your place will help him to come out of his history of beatings and abuse.

If the pet is very young, he needs to be taught the behaviour that is expected out of him. He needs to learn to be sociable. He needs to learn that it is not okay to bite people. There are some tips and tricks that will help you to teach him all this.

Every time the pet tries to bite you, you should loudly say the word 'no'. Do it each time, till the Holland Lop rabbit starts relating the word 'no' to something that he can't do. Don't beat him because this will only scare him. Just be stern with your words and also actions.

If think that the above trick is not very useful, then you can put the pet in his cage for some time. The pet will eventually understand that this behaviour will send him into the cage. The word 'no' and the act of putting him into the cage will make the pet more cautious of his behaviour.

It should be noted that it will take some time for the Holland Lop rabbit to understand this. Until then just be patient and keep repeating these actions each time he tries to nip you. The Holland Lop rabbit will call back on his memory eventually and relate the cage to something punishable.

Another trick to help the Holland Lop rabbit understand that he can't nip and bite is to hold him and drag him away from you. You need to establish the fact that you are the dominant one in the house.

When you are pulling the Holland Lop rabbit away, you need to be very careful. You want to train the pet and not harm him. Use your thumb and the index finger to hold the skin at the back of the Holland Lop rabbit's neck. This skin is loose and you will be able to hold easily.

Look for the reactions of the Holland Lop rabbit. He should not be in pain. The idea is to teach him to give up nipping and biting. When you hold him at the back of his neck, gently push him away from you.

You might have to repeat this action several times before the Holland Lop rabbit understands what is expected of him. The Holland Lop rabbit might also try to give you a good fight when you pull him away.

Don't worry because this is something normal and quite natural of the Holland Lop rabbit. The Holland Lop rabbits play and fight amongst themselves in the natural environment, so he might just try to defend and play with you.

There is another trick that can definitely help your training sessions with the Holland Lop rabbit. You can apply something bitter on your toes and fingers, so that when the Holland Lop rabbit bites you, he gets that bitter taste. When he gets to taste something bitter and terrible on you, he will eventually give up on nipping you.

It is important that the food item that you use is bitter but is not harmful for the Holland Lop rabbit.

There are many treats that the Holland Lop rabbit can lick. You can find these treats online. You can also treat your pet to these foods, so that he can affectionately lick from your hands. You should remember that the Holland Lop rabbit will start ignoring and avoiding you if he only gets to taste bitter stuff from you. Be a teacher to the pet, but remember to be a friendly teacher.

Another point that you need to know while training your pet is that you need to monitor your actions too. You need to figure out whether biting is a habit with the pet or has he suddenly started. If the pet has recently started biting, then it could be something related to you.

Another reason that could be behind your Holland Lop rabbit's biting is that the Holland Lop rabbit could be sick. You have to know your pet well to be able to detect sudden changes in his behaviour. If you see the pet being aggressive when you try to play with him, he could be sick.

You should thoroughly examine your pet for any injuries. If you spot an injury, you should take him to the veterinarian. If he looks sick and tired, even then it is a good idea to take him to the veterinarian. You should never postpone such things because this will drastically affect the pet's health.

Chapter 8: Grooming and showing the Holland Lop rabbit

It is important to groom a Holland Lop rabbit in order to ensure that the coat stays smooth and shiny and the pet stays in the best of health. If you plan to enter your pet bunny into shows, grooming is particularly important. You will have to dedicate time for grooming sessions in order to keep the pet clean and healthy.

1. Grooming the Holland Lop rabbit

You should understand that when you pay attention to the basic cleaning and grooming of the pet rabbit, not only will your pet appear neat and clean; he will also be saved from many unwanted diseases.

When you are looking at grooming sessions for your rabbit, you should pay special attention to the pet's ears, nails, coat, teeth and bathing. This chapter will help you to understand the various dos and don'ts while grooming your pet Holland Lop rabbit.

It should be noted here that the Holland Lop rabbit will not require frequent bathing, but regular brushing of the coat is important to keep the fur in good condition. If you fail to groom the pet regularly, you will put the fur and the skin of the pet at risk.

If you are domesticating the rabbit for its fur or for showing the rabbit, then it is very important that you groom the pet nicely. Grooming the pet rabbit is also necessary to maintain the hygiene and well being of the pet. Even if the pet will not participate in shows, you should make sure that he is neat and clean at all times.

Cleaning the ears

It should be noted that while certain rabbits are prone to various kinds of ear infections, many others aren't. The rabbits with erect ears are less prone to such infections. On the other hand, smaller ears that are not open are more prone to ear infections.

An erect ear type gets enough airflow to save it from infections. Holland Lop rabbits have erect ears. Their ears are open and allow good airflow. While the design of the ears help the Holland Lops rabbit to ward off infections, you also need to do your bit.

It should be noted that wet ears are susceptible to bacteria. The bacteria can grow in the ear and lead to various diseases.

The ears of the Holland Lop rabbit also need to be cleaned regularly so that there is no wax deposited in the ears. There are many owners who might not consider ear cleaning an important part of pet keeping, but in reality wax can lead to mite infestation and other infections.

In severe cases, the hearing power of the pet can be compromised. It is important that you know of the early signs of mite infestation. The wax in the ears will have a light brown color, while the wax with mites will be dark brown in color.

It is important to see the veterinarian in case you have doubts about mite infestations. Don't put any drops in the pet's ears without consulting the vet. In general, you should try to clean the pet's ears once a week, or at least once in ten days.

You will require a cotton swab and an ear cleaning solution that is used for rabbits. If there is somebody in the house who could help you, it will be easier to clean the ears.

If you are the only one doing this task, you should be calm and patient because Holland Lop rabbits don't like their ears being touched and cleaned. You can warm the cleaning solution before use.

Sit comfortably on the floor and hold the Holland Lop rabbit gently by the loose skin behind the neck. Use your lap to give support to the pet's legs. Take a cotton swab and apply some cleaning agent to it.

You should use the cotton swab with the cleaning agent to clean the parts of the ear that are easily visible to you. Don't go too deep because this can hurt the pet. You should definitely not try to go further in the ear canal.

Repeat the process on both the ears. If you commit a small mistake from your side, it could cost the Holland Lop rabbit his hearing. So, you need to make sure that whatever you do is gentle, yet with firm hands.

The Holland Lop rabbit might get uneasy and might try to get away from your grip. To make sure that the pet is stable and not jerking, you can give him a treat. This will keep him occupied and will make your job easier.

Trimming the nails

It is important to cut the nails of the Holland Lop rabbit regularly. You should be looking at doing so at least once a month. If the nails of the Holland Lop rabbit are not cut on a regular basis, there is a chance that the nails will get stuck somewhere. This will cause the nails to get uprooted.

You can imagine the pain your Holland Lop rabbit will have to go through if the nails are uprooted. You will have to rush to the veterinarian to help the Holland Lop rabbit. Not only this, but the long nails can also leave marks and scratches on your skin. So, make it a point to cut the nails of the pet regularly.

You should also make sure that you use the right equipment to cut the nails of the pet Holland Lop rabbit. You should use good quality animal nail clippers. Along with that, you would need soap and styptic powder.

You can give some treats to the pet rabbit. This is to distract the animal so that he does not disturb you when you are busy clipping his nails.

If there is someone else in the house, you can ask them to hold the Holland Lop rabbit. If you're on your own, place the Holland Lop rabbit in your lap in a way that he is comfortable and you have access to his nails.

You will notice a reddish vein on the nail. This is called the quick. You should cut the nail in a way that the quick is not touched. If you happen to hurt it, it will hurt the pet and will also bleed.

In case you cut the nail in way that the quick starts bleeding, use soap to clean it and then apply the powder. This will give relief to the pet. You should give a few minutes to the Holland Lop rabbit to feel better before starting the process of clipping the nails once again.

Cleaning the teeth

Taking care of the teeth is an important part of grooming the Holland Lop rabbit. As the owner of the Holland Lop rabbit, it is important for you to know that the teeth of the rabbit are always growing. If you pay attention you will realize that the teeth sometimes become so big that the rabbit has difficulties in eating.

When you are considering the overall hygiene and cleanliness of the Holland Lop rabbit, you also have to take care of his teeth. You might have problems cleaning the pet Holland Lop rabbit's teeth in the beginning, but he will get used it quickly.

As a rule, you should try to clean the Holland Lop rabbit's teeth once or twice a month. If you ignore his teeth, you will only invite unwanted problems for the Holland Lop rabbit. You will notice tar depositing on the teeth if they are not clean. This will automatically lead to tooth decay.

Many owners complain that the pet closes its mouth while the teeth are being cleaned. This makes it very difficult for the cleaning to take place. If your pet does this, then you can clean only one side of the mouth in one sitting. This means that you will have to be more frequent with the teeth cleaning sessions.

It is also important that you take the pet to the vet if you see any tar on the teeth. Even if all seems fine, it is advised to schedule dental check-ups for the Holland Lop rabbit once or twice a year. The vet will trim the teeth of the pet if there is a need.

To keep the teeth clean on a regular basis, you can find toothpaste specially designed for rabbits. Along with the toothpaste, you should use a soft brush that has been specially designed for them. A toothbrush with hard bristles might hurt the pet's jaw, so you should avoid using it.

Your movements should be very soft. If you are too hard, you will hurt the Holland Lop rabbit. Be very observant of the lather that comes out from the pet's mouth. If you see a pink or red color, you should immediately know that it is blood and that you are being too hard on the bunny's mouth.

Brushing the coat

It should be noted that brushing the coat of the Holland Lop rabbit is essential. You should make sure that you brush the coat of the animal regularly. This will help to ease out the tangles in the hairs of the rabbit.

Regular brushing of the coat will also help you to get rid of dust from the coat. This is important to keep the Holland Lop rabbit neat and clean. You need a brush with soft bristles. Hard bristles can harm the pet, so avoid such a brush. You can buy a good brush online at a cheap price or from a local pet shop near your area.

Holland Lop rabbits have short coats. You need to brush the coat regularly to avoid any fur balls. If you are regular in brushing your rabbit's coat, you automatically eliminate the need to bathe him on a regular basis.

Bathing the Holland Lop rabbit

When you are looking to give a nice bath to your rabbit, you should be looking at two things: a good quality and mild shampoo and a few towels. It is very important that you choose the right shampoo for the Holland Lop rabbit.

If the shampoo is too hard or harsh, it will leave rashes on the rabbit and might even cause serious damage to his skin. This makes it important that you invest in buying a mild shampoo.

You can easily get a good quality shampoo online or in the pet store. Make sure that the shampoo that you choose is very mild on the skin and has proven to be ideal for the Holland Lop rabbit.

You can take a small amount of shampoo and test it on a small part of the skin of the rabbit. This is to make sure that the shampoo is safe for the pet. If you see the skin reacting, then you should make sure that you avoid this shampoo.

You also need a few towels handy for the Holland Lop rabbit. They will help to dry the fur of the pet nicely.

There are a few precautions that you need to take. You should understand that how your rabbit behaves in water will depend on its individual personality. It is important that you make a few attempts to understand your pet's personality. Don't give up and understand his behavior and mannerisms. This will only help you in your future dealings with the pet.

You should always remember that while it is fine to bathe the rabbit once in a while, over-bathing is not recommended. This can also create many problems. The skin of the pet will begin to lose many important essential oils if they are bathed frequently.

If your Holland Lop rabbit is suffering from flea infestation, then you will have to use a shampoo that can help the Holland Lop rabbit get rid of the fleas. You should consult the veterinarian before you use a specialized flea shampoo. It is important not to take a chance on the health of the pet.

It is important that you make a few attempts to understand your pet's personality. Don't give up and understand his behavior and mannerisms. This will only help you in your future dealings with the pet.

To begin with, make sure that the water you are using to bathe the pet is warm. Holland Lop rabbits can get stressed very easily. They will detest cold water. They should be bathed in warm water to keep them safe.

Take a tub and fill it half with warm water. Lift your Holland Lop rabbit delicately in your hands. Make sure that your grip is firm. The pet might surprise you when it touches water and might try to jump out of your hands. To avoid such a situation, place your hands on the stomach area and hold him firmly.

Place the Holland Lop rabbit in the tub of warm water for a few seconds. Observe how he responds to water. If you see him enjoying, then your work becomes easier. You can also sprinkle water over the pet. But, if the pet is not enjoying then you need to be quick.

Take him out of the water, and put some shampoo on his back. You should form a good lather with your hands from the ears towards the tail region. Make sure that the pet does not escape when you are shampooing it. You need to have a firm grip on him.

You can also make use of the kitchen sink to give the rabbit a bath. The sink will be deep and it will be difficult for the bunny to run away. The pet is hydrophobic, so it is advised to use to two sinks or tubs. Fill both with water and use them alternately. Keep talking to your pet and make him feel that everything is fine.

Another way to bathe your hydrophobic Holland Lop rabbit is to sway him under running warm water. Turn the tap on and make sure the water is warm. It should not be cold or too hot. Once you are convinced that the temperature of the water is right for the pet, hold the pet and bring him under the water for a few seconds.

Before he starts to get fidgety, take him away from the water. Now apply some shampoo over the Holland Lop rabbit. Keeping swaying him under the water until all the shampoo is washed off. It is very important that all the shampoo is washed off; else the pet's skin will get affected and will show signs of rashes and abrasions.

After the bath is done, place the bunny in a big towel. You should place a few blankets or towels on the floor to keep it warm and tight for the animal. The Holland Lop rabbit will show too much energy at this time. He will try to escape you. You should be very gentle with the pet, otherwise you could harm him.

While you are bathing the Holland Lop rabbit, it is important that you protect his face. Water should not enter his eyes or ears. These are sensitive areas and water could cause some damage to them. Keep him on the towels and use another towel to pat him dry. Make sure that he is absolutely dry before you let him go, otherwise he will stick dust and dirt on his skin.

Giving a full bath to the Holland Lop rabbit is not an easy job. While it is difficult, it is also not very good for the pet. The pet can get dry skin, which can further lead to many skin related problems and other diseases.

More often than not, the pet owner is forced to give a bath to the Holland Lop rabbit because he has soiled his feet or coat. If you don't clean the feet, the Holland Lop rabbit can soil other areas and can also get an infection.

If you are trying to get rid of this problem, then you can give a footbath instead of a full bath. For a simple footbath, fill a water tub or sink with over half an inch of water. Make the pet walk in the tub or sink. This will help him to get rid of the poopy boots.

You can also wet a big towel or a paper towel and make the Holland Lop rabbit walk on it. You can also use baby wipes if you want to get rid of dirt or a little amount of grime. This is a simple way to avoid a full bath. You can also use these baby wipes to clean off the dirt from this skin and coat.

2. Showing the Holland Lop rabbits

Holland Lop rabbits are adorable pets, but they are capable of being more than just household pets. There are many owners that keep and domesticate Holland Lop rabbits to make them take part in shows. These shows are extensively popular amongst many rabbit lovers.

If you also wish to keep or domesticate the Holland Lop rabbit for the purpose of showing, then you need to make sure that you follow certain guidelines. There are certain breed standards that your Holland Lop rabbit needs to qualify for.

The American rabbit breeders association (ARBA) has set some guidelines that will help you to prepare your Holland Lop rabbits to participate in such shows. You should make sure that you understand these guidelines. These guidelines will help you not just in preparing your rabbit for the show, but also to take good care of the pet.

Rabbit shows give you the opportunity to showcase your rabbit and also win a potential prize. These shows will also help you to meet other rabbit owners. You can connect and exchange notes about your pet animals. This is a great opportunity to broaden your horizons and know more about your breed of rabbit and also other breeds.

It should be noted that you can't suddenly wake up from a slumber and decide to participate in shows. Even if you do so, you will not gain much from the shows. If you are serious about showing your rabbit, then you will have to prepare all year round.

You need to take proper care of the rabbit. You will have to make sure that everything about the bunny is on point. There are many people who take rabbit shows very seriously. They prepare religiously for them. So, it is advised that you prepare well or just quit participating in such rabbit shows.

This chapter will help you understand some breed standards for the Holland Lop rabbits. You will understand how to keep and present the pet in the best possible way. Certain tips for the shows will also be shared. You will learn what needs to be done before the show and on the day of the show.

Breed standards for the Holland Lop rabbits

The BRC has set total 100 points for judging Holland Lop rabbits. Out of these 100 points, 32 points are for body, 10 points for ears, 24 points for head, 5 points for eyes, 8 points for crown, and 10 points are for the feet, legs and bones of the rabbit.

The BRC also has the right to disqualify your rabbit from the rabbit show. The rabbit can be disqualified if it is not healthy or is overdeveloped for its age. It can also be disqualified if it has crooked legs, runny eyes, mutilated teeth, odd color, putty nose, white patches and white armpits.

Preparing for the show

You need to be a member of an organization. The ARBA organization and BRC organization are the two organizations that will allow you to be a member and also enter a show with your Holland Lop rabbit. You can register with either of the two organizations.

The process to become a member is fairly simple and straightforward. You need to approach the organization and show an interest in being their member. You should also register your pet under your Holland Lop rabbit name.

Once you are a member of the organization, you will be intimated with all the latest happenings and shows in your area. You should be alert regarding the requirements and deadlines. The registration process can take some time, so don't wait until the last minute to get it done.

If you want to enter a show with your Holland Lop rabbit, you will have to make sure that your rabbit is in its best form. You should take care of the health and well being of the animal and make sure that he is ready for the contest.

After you are sure that your rabbit is ready to take part in the contest, you can plan on getting him admitted for the show. Always keep checks on the shows happening in your area. You should check if your rabbit fits the requirements.

When you find a show that allows your breed of rabbit to take part in the contest, you should go ahead and register your rabbit. Register your rabbit in the show that you find relevant and suitable.

Though most rules are quite standard, it is always advised to be careful so that your rabbit is not disqualified from the show or subsequent shows. You should also note the deadlines related to the application and other things. It is always better to be prepared before the main show day.

Once you have registered for the show, you need to make sure that you and the pet are ready. Make all the necessary arrangements to get to the venue much before the final day.

After the rabbit is registered to participate in the rabbit show, the wait for the final day begins. You have to ensure that you have all the necessary documents and a copy of the exact schedule with you. You should know the exact time when your bunny would be showed. Having these things handy will help you to avoid the last minute rush and tension.

Conclusion

Thank you again for purchasing this book!

I hope this book was able to help you in understanding the various ways to domesticate and care for Holland Lop rabbits.

Holland Lop rabbits are adorable and lovable animals. These animals have been domesticated for many years. Even though they are loved as pets, they are not very common, and there are still many doubts regarding their domestications methods and techniques. There are many things that prospective owners don't understand about the animal. They find themselves getting confused as to what should be done and what should be avoided.

If you are still contemplating whether you want to domesticate the Holland Lop rabbit or not, then it becomes all the more important for you to understand everything regarding the pet very well. You can only make a wise decision when you are acquainted with all the dos and don'ts and more. When you are planning to domesticate a Holland Lop rabbit as a pet, you should lay special emphasis on learning about its behavior, habitat requirements, dietary requirements and common health issues.

This book will help you to equip yourself with this knowledge. You will be able to appreciate a Holland Lop rabbit for what it is. You will also know what to expect from the animal. This will help you to decide whether the Holland Lop rabbit is the right choice for you or not. If you already have a Holland Lop rabbit, then this book will help you to strengthen your bond with your pet.

Thank you and good luck!

References

http://www.mnn.com

https://en.wikipedia.org

http://www.runningbugfarm.com

http://small-pets.lovetoknow.com

http://www.rabbit.org

http://www.handallhousefarm.com

http://twotalentshomestead.blogspot.in

https://www.popsugar.com

http://ipfactly.com

https://www.petcha.com

http://www.petrabbitinfo.com

https://www.peta2.com

http://www.raising-rabbits.com

http://www.petguide.com

https://joybileefarm.com

https://www.thespruce.com

https://www.pets4homes.co.uk

http://www.hobbyfarms.com

www.training.ntwc.org

http://animaldiversity.org

https://a-z-animals.com

Copyright and Trademarks: This publication is Copyrighted 2018 by Pesa Publishing. All products, publications, software and services mentioned and recommended in this publication are protected by trademarks. In such instance, all trademarks & copyright belong to the respective owners. All rights reserved. No part of this book may be reproduced or transferred in any form or by any means, graphic, electronic, or mechanical, including photocopying, recording, taping, or by any information storage retrieval system, without the written permission of the authors. Pictures used in this book are either royalty free pictures bought from stock-photo websites or have the source mentioned underneath the picture.

Disclaimer and Legal Notice: This product is not legal or medical advice and should not be interpreted in that manner. You need to do your own due-diligence to determine if the content of this product is right for you. The author and the affiliates of this product are not liable for any damages or losses associated with the content in this product. While every attempt has been made to verify the information shared in this publication, neither the author nor the affiliates assume any responsibility for errors, omissions or contrary interpretation of the subject matter herein. Any perceived slights to any specific person(s) or organization(s) are purely unintentional. We have no control over the nature, content and availability of the web sites listed in this book. The inclusion of any web site links does not necessarily imply a recommendation or endorse the views expressed within them. Pesa Publishing takes no responsibility for, and will not be liable for, the websites being temporarily unavailable or being removed from the Internet. The accuracy and completeness of information provided herein and opinions stated herein are not guaranteed or warranted to produce any particular results, and the advice and strategies, contained herein may not be suitable for every individual. The author shall not be liable for any loss incurred as a consequence of the use and application, directly or indirectly, of any information presented in this work. This publication is designed to provide information in regards to the subject matter covered. The information included in this book has been compiled to give an overview of the subject s and detail some of the symptoms, treatments etc. that are available to people with this condition. It is not intended to give medical advice. For a firm diagnosis of your condition, and for a treatment plan suitable for you, you should consult your doctor or consultant. The writer of this book and the publisher are not responsible for any damages or negative consequences following any of the treatments or methods highlighted in this book. Website links are for informational purposes and should not be seen as a personal endorsement; the same applies to the products detailed in this book. The reader should also be aware that although the web links included were correct at the time of writing, they may become out of date in the future.

Made in United States
Troutdale, OR
09/26/2024